Best Tea Shop Walks
on the Isle of Wight

Jacqui Leigh

"All this beauty is of God"
(Tennyson)

Published by Sigma Leisure – an imprint of
Sigma Press, Stobart House, Pontyclerc, Penybanc Road
Ammanford, Carmarthenshire SA18 3HP

British Library Cataloguing in Publication Data

A CIP record for this book is available from the British Library

ISBN: 978-1-85058-893-1

Typesetting and Design by: Sigma Press, Ammanford, Carms

Maps: © Bute Cartographics

Photographs: © Jacqui Leigh

Cover photograph: Freshwater Bay

Printed by: Berforts Group Ltd

Disclaimer: The information in this book is given in good faith and is believed to be correct at the time of publication. Care should always be taken when walking in hill country. Where appropriate, attention has been drawn to matters of safety. The author and publisher cannot take responsibility for any accidents or injury incurred whilst following these walks. Only you can judge your own fitness, competence and experience. Do not rely solely on sketch maps for navigation: we strongly recommend the use of appropriate Ordnance Survey (or equivalent) maps.

Walks

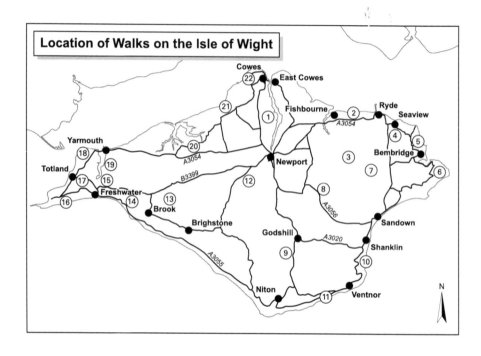

Location of Walks on the Isle of Wight

Foreword

I like walking and I like teashops so I thought, why not combine the two? Since I enjoy both, surely there must be others who do as well, and of course there are. After a good walk in the fresh air I somehow feel I have earned a cup of tea and maybe something tasty to eat. Hence this book.

The Isle of Wight is a wonderful place to walk with 500 miles of footpaths, the highest footpath density in the UK, and numerous teashops in beautiful locations.

The walks in this book vary in length and difficulty; some include at least part suitable for wheelchair users or push-chairs, giving the option of 'there and back' walks, brief notes on this are indicated at the beginning of each walk. The teashops range from the very traditional, with waitresses in black dresses and white aprons, to modern café style establishments with easy chairs and newspapers. Some are teashops only while at the other end of the spectrum some operate as licensed restaurants as well.

Some of the paths are well known and well used but others are less clear and their condition will obviously depend on recent weather conditions. Generally the northern half of the island is heavy clay which can be very claggy if there has been prolonged wet weather; the southern part is mostly chalk which is only of any concern in wet weather as it can be slippery, but it dries quickly. Advice is given at the start of each walk as to the type of path and any special concerns of note.

The information in this book is correct at the time of going to press, legal diversions of paths do take place from time to time but these should be clearly marked.

Jacqui Leigh
April 2011

Please follow the Country code:

- Leave gates as you find them
- Keep your dog under control, especially where stock are grazing (remember farmers can shoot dogs if they are worrying their animals)
- Avoid damaging hedges, fences and walls
- Leave no litter, take it home
- Go carefully on country roads (walk on the right except on sharp bends).

Travel information

Bus
Southern Vectis
01983 827000   www.islandbuses.info
Wightbus
01983 823782   www.iwight.com/wightbus

Rail
Island Line Trains
08457 484950   www.island-line.co.uk
Isle of Wight Steam Railway
01983 884343 (talking timetable)

Map
OS Explorer OL29 Isle of Wight

Walk 1: Cowes, Newport and the River Medina

Level walk around Medina estuary, good for spotting wildlife. The first half is road and cycleway, suitable for wheelchairs and pushchairs with the second half mostly flat footpath. There are frequent buses between Cowes and Newport, so it is possible to walk to Newport and catch the bus back.

The footpath through Seaclose Park, Medina High School and down to the Ryde Queen is usually closed during the Isle of Wight Festival and in the week immediately preceding it. Advice is given in the local newspapers.

Distance	9½ miles/15 km
Start	West Cowes side of the Floating Bridge across the River Medina. Walk along the high street and then down Medina Road to find the Floating Bridge and the beginning of the walk
Parking	Numerous car parks in the town
Getting there by car	The northern end of of the A3020 from Newport
Getting there by bus	Number 1 from Newport stops by the Co-op supermarket

The Walk

From the Floating Bridge walk up Bridge Road and turn left at the mini-roundabout into Arctic Road. The little park on your right is on the site of one of the old railway stations and you will be following the route of the former railway line to Newport.

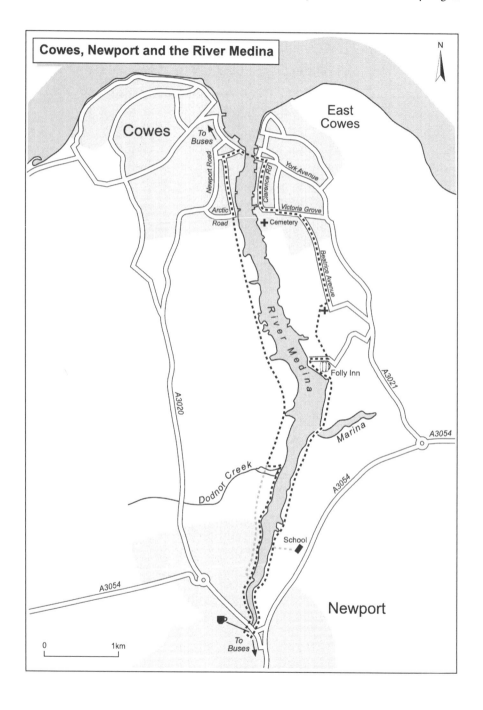

Further along this road, on your left, is the home of the United Kingdom Sailing Academy (UKSA) one of the largest sailing schools in the country. Continue along here for another 600 yards. Just as the road begins to turn uphill to the right you will see the cycleway on your left.

This is a very popular route for both cyclists and walkers, for rambling and for commuting. It is built on the old railway line and you will see several bits of evidence of this in the brick and metal work along the path. There are also places where branches originally went down to the river to allow barges to unload their cargo to the trains for shipment around the Island. Nowadays almost everything is brought over to the Island by truck on the ferries.

The cycleway has, however, become a real wildlife haven. The hedgerow provides a corridor for red squirrels and dormice, although both are very shy. There are lots of little creeks along here making the mud very rich, as a consequence the whole estuary has been given an International and European designation as a feeding ground for wading birds. At low tide you can hear waders of all sorts including the piping call of the oyster-catchers and the liquid sound of the curlews. Much of the bank is protected as high water roosting areas for these birds. The salt marshes are also a protected habitat.

At low tide you will see the remains of many wooden boats sticking up out of the mud like the ribs of some giant animal; a reminder of Cowes and Newport's long maritime history.

Just before the footbridge over Dodnor Creek is Dixon's Copse, a small nature reserve. Take the left turn before the bridge; there is a signpost but it is often hard to see. The footbridge gives lovely views over the Creek, a Site of Special Scientific Interest (SSSI). This is also a good place to watch birds from above.

This footpath takes you away from the cycleway and along the edge of the mill pond, built in the 1790s. Virtually nothing else is left of the mill now. The pond is slightly less saline than the river and has its own eco-system, hence its designation as an SSSI. It is a good place to see ducks, coots, moorhens and little egrets. You may also be lucky enough to see the occasional kingfisher flashing past. There are lots of swans around here and in spring a pair frequently builds its nest on one of the islands in the middle of the pond. The path leads onto a small road past a caravan park.

As the road curves away from the river follow the footpath to your left. This takes you through the grounds of Medina Valley Centre, an environmental education centre and a sailing school, so keep to the footpath (marked with yellow arrows) and watch out for passing dinghies!

About 500 yards further on the path crosses the crane tracks of the Vestas factory, which makes wind turbine blades. These are transported to the mainland on their own special barges called, appropriately enough, Blade Runner to be sold abroad.

Continue along the path, past Newport Rowing Club, founded in 1863. Go past the picnic tables and straight on to the mermaid guarding the little bridge. Carry on over the footbridge and along a short section of path out onto a road. Go straight ahead, past Odessa Boatyard, a small independent boatyard with its own mini lighthouse. Keep to the riverside and carry on to the end of the road. Turn left here and into the Quay Arts Centre. The café is through the shop.

On leaving the building, turn left and left again to find yourself on the opposite quay, in the area known as Newport Harbour.

On the cycle-way you may or may not have noticed that there are several apple trees. Local legend has it that these have grown from the discarded apple cores thrown from train carriage windows, but this is a myth because the trees are too young. In fact there are some quite unusual varieties growing along here and their origin lies in the section of path just after the crane tracks. Here are the remains of orchards and gardens of a house which used to belong to the owner of a local nursery. In order to safeguard his stock he kept examples of many cultivars in his own garden, in case disease or other problems affected his main stock at the nursery some miles away in Godshill. Birds have carried the seeds along the path and even to the other side of the river.

Newport Harbour, the end of the navigable part of the river

This was once a busy commercial port as the buildings opposite suggest and led to the town's dominance in the 1900s. The introduction of larger ships, and the desire to be able to land goods regardless of the tide, led to its slow decline. However in recent years the harbour has seen a resurgence of use by leisure sailors. In summer it is a popular haunt for those that can 'take the bottom' (those that can rest on the mud without damage). In the winter the wall is lined with boats, which have been lifted out so that their owners can work on them.

Continue through this area, then past Jubilee Stores, now used as artists' workshops. Other warehouses along here have been converted into a Bus Museum and the Classic Boat Museum. The footpath actually goes off to the right just before the Bus Museum but you can rejoin it further on opposite the Travelodge.

The footpath takes you through Seaclose Park and then Medina High School grounds, now the location of the Isle of Wight Festival, which has seen performances by the Police, The Rolling Stones, KT Tunstall, Snow Patrol , Paul McCartney, to name a few. The Festival was revived in 2002 after a gap of thirty two years and takes place annually in

June. Occasionally, you may see one of the large rescue helicopters putting down here as this is the point of transfer to and from ambulances.

Keep to the riverside here as the other path goes up through Medina Arboretum to the main road. After one and a half miles you will find yourself walking past the rusting hulk of a paddle steamer.

The Ryde Queen was built in 1933 and saw valiant service crossing the Solent for many years. She was brought to the Medina in 1969 to be used as a nightclub. She was floated in and then walled up using concrete in sacks, over which you are now walking. Sadly she was gutted by fire in 1977 and cost too much to restore, so she has been left to decay where she is.

The footpath continues over the lock gates at the entrance to Island Harbour. A mile further on you will reach the Folly Inn where you need to head up Folly Lane for 300 yards to rejoin the footpath on your left, at the bend in the road. The path goes through the copse and across a field to Whippingham Church.

Dedicated to St Mildred, an Anglo-Saxon Princess, the foundations of Whippingham Church date from before the Norman Conquest in 1066. However the present church was designed by Prince Albert, and built in 1860 for use as a royal chapel. The church contains the chair that Queen Victoria used when she attended services, and a candelabrum given by her to the church. Osborne House, her favourite holiday residence, is less than a mile away. Opposite the church are the Almshouses. These were built under the instruction of Queen Victoria for retired Royal servants. This area features in the film 'Mrs Brown', about the later life of Queen Victoria.

The path takes you alongside the churchyard and on to Beatrice Avenue to East Cowes to your left. The most straightforward way is to follow this road past the school until it joins the larger Victoria Grove, then turn left and follow the main road down through the town towards the chain ferry. Alternatively, you can follow the road past the school, but turn left onto a footpath just past Greenlands Road and work your way down to the river. This route will take you through the marina and past the RNLI Inshore Centre, which services all the

St Mildred's Church, Whippingham

inshore boats and engines for the whole country.

Whichever route you take, you should end up at the chain ferry or 'floating bridge' as it is known locally.

There has been a floating bridge here since 1859 and the one currently in use is the eighth such vessel.

As you cross the river you will see the large black crane, in what was once JS White's yard, where Barnes Wallis, designer of the Wellington Bouncing Bomb (Dambusters), served as an apprentice. Surprisingly, for such a small town, this shipyard was able to build anything up to the size of a minesweeper or a small frigate. In the Second World War it provided a vital repair facility for the naval ships of many countries. One such ship was the Blyskawica which, in 1942, repaid the town by defending it from a German bombing raid. Since then, there have been regular links with Poland and there is a thriving Blyskawica Society.

The short crossing will bring you back to West Cowes, where there are numerous cafes, and the end of the walk

The Quay Arts Café
Open all year 9am - 5pm
Tel: 01983 528825

Although not cheap, the café has an interesting and constantly changing menu, including vegetarian and gluten free options. The range of cakes is small but they are freshly made on the premises and, again, there are often gluten-free options. There are also plenty of other snacks to try. You can sit outside on the quay itself or inside in the cool airy café with pieces of art work on the walls. The tea is served in sensible sized pots and the coffee is good although the espresso is not very strong.

The original idea behind the redevelopment of these former Mew Langton Brewery buildings was to show-case the work of local artists, and the exhibitions are housed in the café and the various rooms leading off it. The centre also has its own small theatre and cinema, and the shop sells ceramics, jewellery and cards, again by local artists.

Walk 2:
Fishbourne and Quarr

First half flat walking on a bridleway, suitable for wheelchairs but a bit bumpy in places. Option of return along beach with suitable tides, in which case old trainers are better than walking boots as there is soft clay in places.

Check the tides if you are going to do the second half of this walk, back along the beach.

Distance	2½ or 3 miles/4 or 5 km
Start	Church Road, Binstead
Parking	Park in Church Road, Binstead which is off the roundabout at the top of Quarr Hill. An alternative is to park in Fishbourne Lane and walk along the beach first then back via the bridleway
Getting there by car	Binstead is on the A3054 Newport to Ryde road. Church Road is at the western end of the village
Getting there by bus	Bus numbers 4 from East Cowes and 9 from Newport, both going to Ryde, stop at the end of Church Road

The Walk

As you head along Church Road look out for Quarr Road, on your left, to begin the walk This road eventually turns into a bridleway, R3, leading straight through to Fishbourne.

About 10 yards before you reach the first gate look down at your feet and you will see two poems set into the path. They were put there for

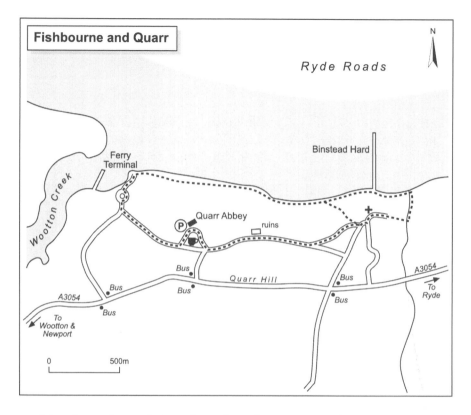

an Island arts festival. Somehow these have survived. On the gate itself is a poetry box which anyone can put contributions in. The board next to it displays some efforts received.

A little further on the path goes through the old mediaeval abbey, destroyed at the command of Henry VIII in the Dissolution. On your left were the fish ponds and on your right the main buildings, the first of which was the infirmary chapel, built over the little stream which although small, is surprisingly reliable. The toilet facilities would have been at this end of the abbey, nearest the sea – no doubt a bit smelly, but up-to-the-minute hygiene of the day, when much went into the middle of the street. The larger building, now converted into barns and a house, was the refectory. As you can see, the abbey was quite extensive and the bridle path you are standing on passes over the site of the main church.

The name 'Quarr' derives from an old term for a stone outcrop. You have already passed the quarry used here, a shallow pit dug in the hillside to extract the stone which lies in the area before the old enclosure wall. This low-lying area is not an obvious place for an abbey, which owned several properties on the island. Without the Ryde to Newport road, it would have been very secluded, and the proximity to the sea allowed them to maintain contact with Normandy. Because of course, like most abbeys of this age, it was founded by a Norman lord, in this case Baldwin de Redvers in 1132, fourth Lord of the Island. The Abbey was closed down almost 400 years later, in 1536, and much of the best dressed stone was taken from this and other abbeys to build Henry VIII's defences at Yarmouth and Cowes.

A little further on you will come to the new monastery with its impressive abbey church completed in 1912. The tea rooms are in the abbey gardens.

Quarr Abbey, a Benedictine Monastery

Quarr Abbey

The abbey is built of hard Belgian brick which is why it looks as if it were finished yesterday. The monks here originally came from Solesmes in France from whence they were driven by the persecution experienced in that country at the time. They originally moved into the vacant Appuldurcombe House in the south of the Island, but were then given the house on this site by a Catholic family who owned the old abbey lands. Gradually they were able to build themselves an abbey large enough for nearly a hundred monks to live and work in, although today there are only about 30. The Abbey has a beautiful garden area which you can walk in, surrounded by an orchard and a vegetable garden. Sometimes there are chickens running around in the orchard. There are pigs and sheep too as agriculture is still an important part of monastic life here: they try to be as self-sufficient as possible.

The church is open to the general public and is worth a visit. The high, vaulted, interior is unadorned but has a simple beauty of its own. There are short services at 2.20pm and 5pm where you can listen to the plainchant of the monks. It has a wonderful, peaceful atmosphere: just to sit there for a few minutes is a restorative to the soul.

After the abbey rejoin the path and continue to Fishbourne. The fields to your right are great places to see kestrels hovering: searching for small mammals. When you reach the end of the lane turn right and head down to the sea.

The Fishbourne to Portsmouth car ferry departs from here and it is quite interesting to watch it make its way through its very narrow navigation channel, especially at low tide. The furthermost house on the shore is built atop much older stone walls and, in fact, the old abbey originally owned this land and had a quay here where they could land fish, hence the place name, and send out their wool.

From the end of the road you can see back down the river to the Sloop where the monks' mill once stood, for which they built the original bridge over the creek. They continued to maintain it up until the Dissolution when responsibility passed to the local authorities.

In the summer there are often people sailing here as this creek is also home to the Royal Victoria Yacht Club.

If you are going back along the beach, having checked the tides, be careful on the first part as there is clay under the sand which can be very sticky if recently wet. Once past the rocks the upper beach is firm and fairly easy to walk along, although littered with dead trees, the result of mini land slips as the soft clay is eroded by tide and rain.

Even in Roman times the land extended considerably further out than it does now and as you walk look out for traces of a medieval village on the sea shore.

The mud flats at low tide provide a rich feeding area for waders and other seabirds. You should be able to see pied oyster-catchers,

Thatched house on Church Road

redshank, little dunlin, shelduck and cormorants as well as many others. It is also an area rich in fossils and other relics of the past. At the end of the last Ice Age the Solent was a river running through a forest stretching out past where you are now standing and fossilized animal remains have been found on this beach.

The more modern sights visible are Ryde pier, the first pier in the world to be built, although the original pier was wooden. Before it was built travellers to the island had to be carried ashore on the backs of porters. It is still in use as a passenger landing pier today. On the opposite shore is Spinnaker Tower, in Portsmouth. It was supposed to be built for the Millennium but was not actually completed until 2005! To the west, the chimney of Fawley power station is clearly visible. The two provide very useful landmarks for sailors. You will also see large ships arriving from all over the world making their way to Southampton docks.

After about a mile and a half, just near the remains of an old jetty, there are wooden steps up from the beach, through a wildlife area, back to Quarr Road. However, if tides permit, you can continue further

Sheela-na-Gigs

Sheela-na-Gigs are figurative carvings of naked women displaying an exaggerated vulva. They are found on churches, castles and other buildings, particularly in Ireland and Britain, sometimes together with male figures. Ireland has the greatest number of known Sheela-na-Gig carvings but there are several across Britain including the one at Holy Cross church, Binstead.

The purpose of them is unclear; one theory is that, like gargoyles, they are meant to ward off death and evil and keep evil spirits away. They are often positioned over doors or windows, presumably to protect these openings, and in this case over a gateway. They are very ugly, by medieval standards, which suggests that they may have been used to represent female lust as hideous and sinfully corrupting. Yet another theory is that they are remnants of a pre-Christian fertility or Mother Goddess religion, carved on to structures, later converted for Christian worship.

until you reach a place where a stream flows out onto the beach near
a corrugated iron shed with several boats in a fenced off compound.
The path is between the compound and the stream. When you reach
the other end of the path turn right onto a bridleway called Ladies
Walk, probably dating from the time when ladies took a promenade
especially after church on Sunday. The bridleway leads to the twelfth
century church of the Holy Cross.

*The church contains a pre-reformation bell in the bell tower, which
probably came from the old Quarr Abbey. In 1969 the church was
seriously damaged by fire and required major restoration work. As you
pass look for a 'Sheela-na-gig', known locally as the Saxon Idol, carved
on the stone gateway to the churchyard.*

The bridleway becomes a road as it reaches the church. Follow this
road round to the left and after 20 yards take the right turn back into
Church road which is the road that the walk began in.

Quarr Abbey Tea Rooms
Open all year, weekdays 10.30am-4pm, Sundays 11.00am-4pm
(may close earlier in winter)

This must be one of the few cafés managed by a monk, and certainly
the only one on the Island. It is staffed mainly by volunteers so
opening times may vary occasionally. As well as the chairs inside,
there are seating areas outside on the hard standing and across the
lawn under the delightful arbours. Although the cakes are limited in
variety they are usually home made in the abbey kitchens. The service
is always friendly and kind and the prices are very reasonable and
there is a relaxed, unhurried atmosphere.

There is also a shop selling cards, religious books and pottery made
by one of the monks. The monks of the abbey have a fine reputation
for bookbinding and repairs and occasionally they have displays of
their work, including beautiful gold tooling. The bookshop has moved
around to various locations but it is certainly worth looking for.

Walk 3:
Ashey to Havenstreet

Easy walking on footpaths, 50 yards on a main road. A pleasant, country walk including a ride on a steam train.

Distance	5 miles/8km
Start	Havenstreet Steam Railway Station
Parking	Havenstreet Steam Railway Station has a large free car park
Getting there by car	Havenstreet is 3 miles south west of Ryde and 3 miles east of Newport. The station is at the southern end of Havenstreet village
Getting there by bus	Wightbus numbers 29 and 33 from Ryde

You will need to check the times of trains in advance but the ticket, once bought, allows you to ride up and down the line all day if you wish. Information is available online at: www.iwsteamrailway.co.uk or from Isle of Wight Tourist Information Offices.

Take the train to Ashey Station (you will need to tell the guard in advance that you wish to alight there). At Ashey Station leave the platform and go back to the level crossing, where there is a footpath sign. Take footpath R28 towards Ashey Down. Follow the hedge for about two thirds of a mile to a main road (Ashey Road). Just before the road is a bricked up tunnel, which is part of the old tramway used to carry chalk from the nearby pits to Ashey Station, the hedge following the line of the tramway.

Once on the road, turn right for 50 yards, then right again at the start of the copse, onto the public footpath (R22, but not numbered at this end). Make your way across the field, almost parallel to the road, in the direction of the signpost to the hedge, turn right and follow the

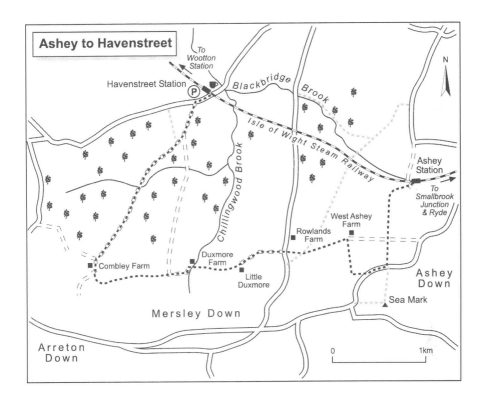

hedge to the stile by West Ashey Farm. It is hard to distinguish the path from the cattle tracks but you need, eventually, to end up in the corner of the field nearest the farm. Cross this stile, then the second on the other side of the track. On your left is another pair of stiles with a plank bridge in between. Cross these and follow the hedge on your left towards the gate at the other end of this field. Once through the gate, go up a small incline, straight across the next field, with a hedge on your right, this time to the finger post by a gate into a small lane.

In the lane turn left for a few yards and take footpath R13, to Little Duxmore, which follows a fairly newly made farm track. At the bottom of the dip the track crosses a small stream. At this point the track turns right, but on the left is the footpath going between the stream and 'The Old Barn'. Follow this path and, about 50 yards after the house, look for a footpath on the right, indicated by a yellow arrow

Havenstreet Station

on a gate. Go though here and follow the path across the fields, following the line of telegraph poles, then along a track for a quarter of a mile to Duxmore Farm.

Just after Lilac Cottage is a T-junction. Turn left and follow the track around to the right for a further 200 yards, whereupon it meets another track. Go straight ahead here across the field opposite, there is a footpath arrow but it is hidden under the ivy. Continue in this direction for about half a mile on fairly level ground.

Suddenly you realise there is a sharp dip in front of you. At this point stop and turn right through the gate down towards the farm buildings at the bottom. Go on past the farm leaving the house on your left, through a gate marked with a yellow arrow and turn right onto a track, which is the bridleway back to Havenstreet, 1½ miles away. This brings you out at the bottom end of Havenstreet Station Car Park. Your ticket allows you access back into the station where the café is.

Granny Winter's Pantry, Havenstreet Station
Open when the station is open
Talking timetable: 01983 884343
www.iwsteamrailway.co.uk

Havenstreet Station is the focal point for the Isle of Wight Steam Railway and houses not only the café but also a small museum, a shop and the engineering workshop. The trains running here are composed mostly of Island stock, which has been lovingly restored by enthusiastic and dedicated volunteers.

At first glance the café building looks like the other buildings in the station, and you would be forgiven for thinking that it is a similar age. Actually it was built in the 1980s, under a youth opportunities scheme, but has been cleverly designed to blend in. The café serves cakes, hot and cold snacks and ice-cream. The range of cakes is fairly small because they are freshly made by one of the volunteers. The service is very cheery and friendly, giving you the feeling that nothing would be too much trouble. A pleasant way to relax, either watching the trains coming and going, or the people travelling on them.

Ashey Station

Walk 4:
Seaview

Easy walking on farmland and Coastal Path. Views across the Solent.

Seaview became very popular in Victorian times and even had its own pier for steamships from the mainland, to bring fashionable people to an exclusive resort. It continued to be popular into the twentieth century and once boasted three banks, several butchers, grocers and bakers, as well as antiques shops. Now there are just a couple of shops and a small post office, however, it remains a very expensive place to live with a lot of properties used as holiday homes. In the summer it is a bustling seaside resort and has its own regatta, which includes sailing, rowing, swimming and a greasy pole competition, as well as lots of beach games. In winter it is transformed into a tranquil place where the residents enjoy a more relaxed way of life.

Distance	5½ miles/9 km
Start	Seaview car park
Parking	Free car park in the village
Getting there by car	Coming from Ryde on the B3330 turn left at Nettlestone Green onto the B3340 to Seaview
Getting there by bus	Number 8 from Ryde and Sandown stops in the middle of the village

The Walk

Starting from the car park, head down Pier Road. Follow the road down to the sea. At the end of the sea wall turn right by The Old Boathouse, then left onto a gravelled road. At the end of this road take

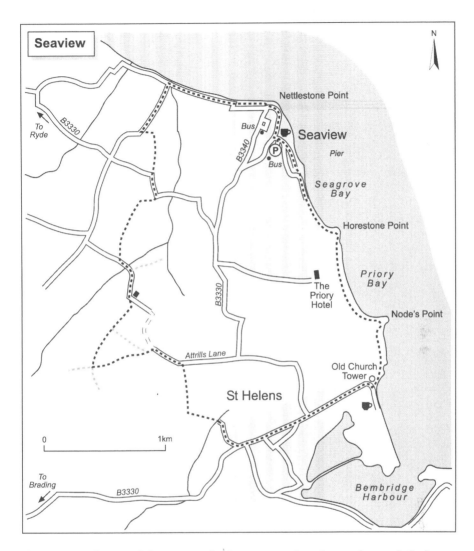

the narrow footpath between the houses and at the end turn left down the road to Seagrove Bay. This leads onto a promenade to your right. At the end of the promenade a walkway takes you into a tiny piece of National Trust land; follow the path through here down to the beach. It is necessary to walk along the beach as the next section of woodland is private and belongs to Priory Bay Hotel, but as you reach the far end of the little wall delineating the hotel grounds, there is a footpath sign pointing up into Priory Woods giving you the option of continuing round the bay along the beach, if the tide is low, or taking a delightful woodland walk.

From here on the beach you get a good view of the sea forts built to protect Portsmouth against a French invasion. The gap between island and mainland is much wider here than at the other end of the Solent and the solution was to build four forts, known locally as Palmerston's Follies, because the Prime Minister's fears that lay behind their construction proved unfounded. However they did come into use in the Second World War. Wooden barriers were built from the shore out to the middle two forts, then a boom was slung across the gap which could be raised and lowered to prevent enemy submarines entering the Solent.

St Helen's is the smallest of the four Solent forts and still in private ownership, since being sold off by the Crown Estates in 1982. It was up

Seagrove bay

for sale in 2003 for £200,000. The forts have their own artesian wells supplying water from an aquifer below the sea bed.

After about a quarter of a mile the woodland path eventually leads back down to the beach for a few yards, then on to the sea wall in St Helens.

When you reach the remains of the old, 12th century, St Helens church (all that is left is the tower) turn right up Duver Road, if you are not going to the Baywatch Beach Café. There are public toilets next to the café.

The Duver Road leads up the hill past the old church lodge. At the top of the hill go straight ahead and continue along this road past the Green. As you walk, look out for the home of Sophie Dawes (see below for details of her life) and, a little further on, the Little Shell House, one wall of which is decorated with shells and bits of glass, and even includes a map of the Isle of Wight.

The 'Queen of Chantilly'

Sophie Dawes, nick-named the Queen of Chantilly, was the daughter of an alcoholic fisherman named Richard Daw. She grew up in the workhouse at Newport and, after a short period of employment with a local farmer, worked as a chambermaid in Portsmouth, then ran away to London where she worked as a servant in a high-class brothel. Here, she eventually became the mistress of the duc de Bourbon, afterwards Prince of Condé. The Duke had her educated in London and then took her to Paris. To prevent scandal, and to qualify her to be received at court, he had her married in 1818 to Adrien Victor de Feuchères, a major in the Royal Guards. The prince provided her dowry, made her husband his aide-de-camp and a baron. She was ambitious and manipulative, a real 'gold-digger' and became a person of consequence at the court of Louis XVIII, but later fell out of favour. After the death of her lover, in strange circumstances, and the Revolution in France, she returned to London to live on her inheritance. She died in 1840. Not bad for the daughter of a semi-literate smuggler.

The old St Helen's Church

Continue on along here for half a mile until you reach Field Lane on your right, signposted footpath R77, to Attrill's Lane. Just a few yards up here bear left along West Green. At the end of this lane turn left, still following Footpath R77, and go over the stile, then keep to the field edge. After the stile, at the other end of the field, bear slightly right. The path goes straight across the middle of the field and is well worn. On the other side of this field cross the stile and turn left into Attrill's Lane, a very common local name, following the lane for about 200 yards. Where the track divides, take the left-hand path but stay on the track, don't turn into the field.

This is good arable land here and it is beautiful to watch little cats' paws of breeze rippling through golden fields of wheat.

Continue along this track for another 200 yards round the edge of the fields. At the next junction turn right onto bridleway B12 with the hedge on your left.

These wide, open fields are home to hares, with their black tipped ears, as well as the more familiar, commonplace rabbits. Larks sing high up above and yellow hammers, wrens and various warblers populate the hedges.

After a further 200 yards you will reach Park Farm. Continue on past the farm house down to a small bridge. About 100 yards after the bridge turn right onto bridleway R61. Follow this through a couple of gates, round a garden then down the drive of Westbourne Cottage to a main road, Pondwell Hill. Cross over and turn left for about 100 yards, then take the footpath R59, by The Wishing Well pub. At the end of the path turn right onto a small road and follow the road down to the sea, past Seaview Wildlife Encounter, a tourist attraction which is famous for its flamingos and also a breeding colony of Humboldt penguins.

When you reach the seafront turn right and walk along the duver (a local dialect term for sand dunes). At low tide there are acres of sand – an excellent place for flying kites! At the end of the Duver Road is a small path, with a sign indicating Coastal Path, along the sea wall round Seaview Yacht Club, to the Esplanade. Follow this road round the corner up the High street to the Copper Kettle, almost opposite the Seaview Hotel.

The Baywatch Beach Café
Open April to October 10am-9pm
Tel: 01983 873259

This is one of the pricier establishments in this book. It has the typical, relaxed feel of a beach café, with tables on the sea wall and gay parasols, serving snacks, hot meals and ice-creams. They have recently extended their menu to include evening meals and have a reasonable reputation for seafood. The tea and coffee comes in mugs and it is also licensed. Most of the food is not homemade but it is good quality and the portions are generous. Its great location means it is popular with visitors and locals alike.

The Copper Kettle, Seaview
Opening hours: Summer 9.30am-4.30pm; Winter 10am-3pm
Tel: 01983 612230

The Copper Kettle has probably the most 'teashoppy' feel of all the premises in this book. It is a traditional tea room, serving proper leaf tea, in china teapots and with beautiful crockery. Their standard tea is Carisbrooke blend but they also offer a very large selection of other teas and tisanes. They serve fresh well made cakes and as well as other snacks and light meals, all tastefully presented by friendly local staff. It is also a licensed restaurant serving good home-prepared food and local wine and beer.

The Copper Kettle occupies what used to be the dining room of Stansfield House, a guest house where, anecdotally, Edward VIII stayed on his last night before his abdication. Unsurprisingly this is very popular in the summer. The only drawbacks are that it is quite small and there is no outside seating, so it can get quite crowded.

Walk 5:
St Helens

Very varied terrain, some steep. Includes walk round harbour and through nature reserve and red squirrel habitats.

Distance	6½ miles/10.5km
Start	The Green, St Helens
Parking	There are places to park around the Green. If you don't mind paying, there is parking down on the Duver by the Baywatch Café or in the National Trust car park behind it, cross the Duver to the harbour's edge and start from*
Getting there by car	St Helens is on the B3330 between Ryde and Brading
Getting there by bus	Number 8 from Ryde and Sandown

The Walk

Start in St Helens at the eastern end of The Green and head east towards the Duver Road. The road is signed to the Baywatch café and there is a nicely illustrated information board at the top of the hill. About 30 yards from the top, take footpath R88 on the right down the hill through St Helens Common to The Duver.

A duver is an Isle of Wight dialect term for an area of sand dunes; this one was used as a links golf course until 1963, the first golf course on the Island and patronised by the future King George V when he wasn't sailing at Cowes, the old clubhouse is still here on the north side.

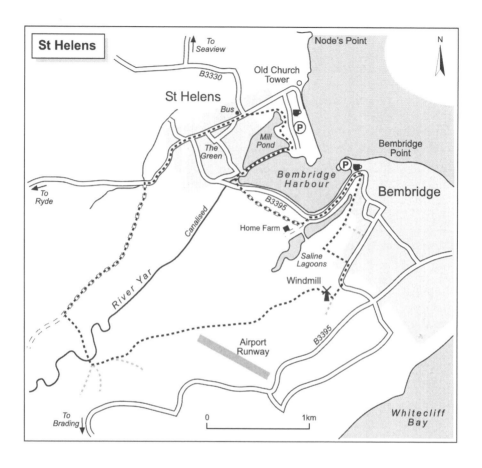

Nowadays The Duver is owned and maintained by the National Trust and is a great place to observe migrant birds on passage to and from other parts of the country.

At the bottom of the hill turn right over the footbridge onto the Duver. Follow the path as it curves round to the right, skirting the marshy extremities of the harbour, to eventually reach a narrow causeway.

In the summer this area is covered with thrift or sea pink.

*The walk now crosses the causeway that separates the old mill ponds from the rest of the harbour.

St Helen's Mill is at the far end and was a tide mill. One wonders why the idea of using the free power of the tides went out of favour for so long. Maybe such mills will have a part to play again in the future.

When you leave the causeway, go past the rebuilt mill on your right then turn left over the bridge. Continue past the Selwyn Court Marine Apartments then turn left into the small car park and over the little footbridge crossing the entrance to Brading Canal.

This was once a busy waterway carrying many of the Island's goods to and from Portsmouth.

Cross this second parking area then cross the road and go down the left-hand track opposite. After a few yards you will see a sign saying Brading Marsh Nature Reserve.

Along this lovely little path you can see and hear all manner of wildlife including greenfinches, yellow hammers, swallows and reed buntings; the saline lagoons are also home to little egrets and the rare starlet sea anemone.

At the end of the the path turn left up a track to the road then turn right and follow the road round the harbour, past Brading Haven Yacht Club and some houseboats, which include converted barges, cruisers and even an old gunboat!

If the tide is high you are quite likely to see people 'messing about in boats' as Ratty would have it, some may be racing, some just pottering about. Dinghy sailing is very popular in the shelter of the harbour and you may also see some Bembridge Redwings, which have been sailing here since 1897. Their name comes from their red sails and they were designed specifically for the shallow waters and shoals of the Harbour.

The Zambezi houseboat

Causeway between Bembridge harbour and the mill pond

On the south side of the harbour is Toll Gate Café if you want to take your refreshment now rather than wait to the end.

As the road turns uphill away from the harbour, take the road to the right, Station Road, next to the Pilot Boat Inn. This turns into a track and then, as the houses end, a footpath. At the next junction go straight ahead into Brading Marsh Nature Reserve, which is both beautiful and peaceful at any time of the year. Follow the main path through the Nature Reserve for about 400 yards, then up hill to the left as it leaves the reserve. At the top, turn right onto the road for about a third of a mile. Take care along here as there is no footway for the last 200 yards and the road is fairly busy. Rejoin the path at Bembridge Windmill. Go along the track, which is signposted BB36 but the sign is often obscured by vegetation, past Mill Farm then turn right onto footpath BB21, leaving the windmill on your left (again the sign is difficult to see). Go through the gate and across the field.

From here you get a good view of Bembridge Airport, home to the world famous Britten Norman Islander, which is the best-selling commercial aircraft produced in Western Europe.

The embankment is actually part of the old sea wall dating from before the land was drained for the railway in the late 19th century.

St Helen's Beach

The tide goes out a long way here and it is good for rock -pooling. On some days it is low enough to walk out to St Helens fort, the nearest of the four sea forts built to defend the Solent and Portsmouth from invaders. You will also see here the remains of St Helens church, built in the 12th Century but abandoned in 1703 when it began to fall into the sea. It was bricked up but the tower was kept as it had long been used as a seamark. It is reputed to be the last sight of England that Nelson had, when the Victory was anchored to collect fresh water. The derelict church didn't go unused: dressed stones from its walls, which were soft sandstone, were found to be good for scrubbing the decks of wooden planked warships – hence the terms 'holystones' and 'holystoning the decks'.

Bembridge windmill

Some care is needed on this part of the walk: the first bit is across National Trust land then over an embankment through marshes and then across the airfield itself. After the airfield the path (BB20) crosses another couple of fields before re-entering Brading Marsh Nature Reserve. The path then leads down into a small wooded area known as Centurion's Copse, perhaps betokening Brading's Roman Past, although no-one really knows the origin of the name. At the clearly marked junction, turn right towards Brading following BB23, then right again at the junction by the information board.

There are red squirrels in this copse but they are very shy and you are most likely to see them if you are on your own. I have most often been made aware of their presence by a 'tutting' which sounds as if they are scolding you for walking through their woods.

After 200 yards turn right again at the next junction and cross the former lock, showing how the Yar was canalized to make it navigable, allowing the boats to remain this far up when the tide went out. After the second bridge, keep to the right around the edge of the fields. When you reach the houses turn right into footpath B2 to St Helens.

This is the end of Quay Lane and, until the railway embankment was built and the land drained in 1894, the sea came in this far and goods were shipped to and from the rest of England and abroad.

After 50 yards, the path leads onto the former branch railway line B56, which is signposted but not numbered at this end. Continue on this track for about a mile, which eventually bears left to the road. Turn right here and walk up hill to St Helen's and the village green, where an annual village fair is still held. If you want refreshment you can follow the signs at the other end of The Green back down to Baywatch Beach Café on the Duver where there is parking.

The Toll Gate Café, Bembridge
Open all year, Oct to April 10am-4pm, May to September 10am-5pm
Tel.: 01983 872992

This is one of the establishments in this book that cannot really be described as a 'tea room'. It has the bizarre feel of a transport café transplanted to the seaside and yet it has the relaxed and unpretentious feel of a family run business, which it is. It is open seven days a week until 4pm in the winter and later in the summer. You can get a variety of snacks and simple, but substantial, home cooked meals here. And I can definitely recommend the hot puds and ice-cream. Tea and coffee comes in cups or mugs and the slab cakes come ready wrapped, so are ideal to take away. Sitting outside watching the comings and goings of a busy harbour on a sunny day is a real joy. Rather quirkily the café also sells souvenirs, postcards, sweets, toys, cross-stitch kits and second-hand books – something for everyone.

The Baywatch Beach Café
Open April to October 10am-9pm
Tel. 01983 873259

This is one of the pricier establishments in this book. It has the typical, relaxed feel of a beach café, with tables on the sea wall and gay parasols, serving snacks, hot meals and ice-creams. They have recently extended their menu to include evening meals and have a reasonable reputation for seafood. The tea and coffee comes in mugs and it is also licensed. Most of the food is not homemade but it is good quality and the portions are generous. Its great location means it is popular with visitors and locals alike.

Walk 6:
Bembridge

Coastal walk. Beach options, steep in parts and can be muddy. Goes through a nature reserve.

Distance	4½ miles/7km
Start	By the Toll Gate Café
Parking	There is a small gravelled parking area next to the Toll Gate Café on the south side of Bembridge harbour
Getting there by car	Take the B3395 to the south side of the harbour
Getting there by bus	Bus no 8 from Ryde and Sandown stops right by the Toll Gate Cafe

The Walk

If the tide is not too high, it isn't too far to walk along the beach as far as the lifeboat station and there are places to rejoin the path along the way. Go to the beach along the track next to the parking area and walk south, away from the harbour. Otherwise take the right-hand of the two footpaths on the bend opposite the Pilot Boat Inn, marked Private Road and Coastal Path but with no number.

Follow the blue Coastal Path signs, passing through a very well-to-do area with large houses set in beautiful grounds; this part of the town has remained a maze of private roads, mostly unmade. About a quarter of a mile after East Cliff house the Coastal Path is signed to the left, follow this to the shore and descend the steps to join the more adventurous on the beach. The lifeboat house on the end of its pier should now be visible. 200 yards further on there is a good path

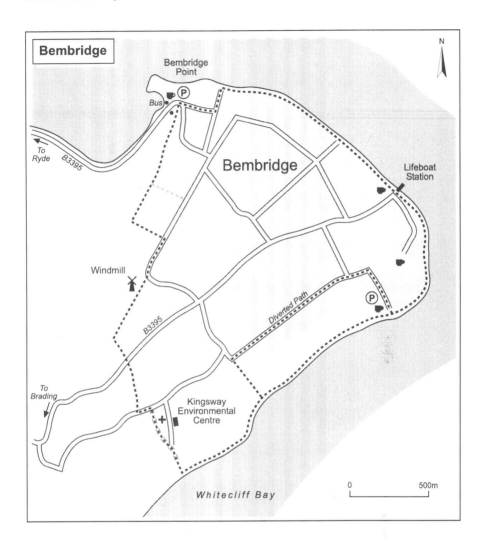

along the seawall which brings you out to Bembridge Lifeboat Station, one of two RNLI stations on the Island, the other is at Yarmouth.

Bembridge has a Tamar Class all-weather lifeboat at the end of the pier and a RIB in the shed next to the shop. These are often open in the summer and they welcome visitors. There are two alternative refreshment places here, if you want to stop half way, one just before the station, The Lifeboat View, and one after, The Bembridge Coast Hotel.

To continue the walk go down the steps just beyond the pier and walk along the seawall.

You can frequently see cheery little pied wagtails hopping about on the rocks. Bembridge Ledge is marked at high tide by permanently choppy water but at low tide it is a great place for rock-pooling; you can also see the remains of nineteenth century salt pans when the tide is out. Further out you can see Nab Tower rising up out of the sea.

If you are going to the Bembridge Coast Hotel, at the end of the sea wall turn right up some steps, and then left through the grounds of the hotel to find the paved area outside the café. Otherwise continue along the beach for about three-quarters of a mile.

Bembridge lifeboat pier

The Nab Tower

The story of the Nab's origin goes back nearly a century. In the early part of 1918 attacks by German U-boats on the British merchant fleet caused the Admiralty so much anxiety that it was decided to take counter measures and an unusual plan was drawn up by 'backroom' scientists. This plan was to sink a line of eight fort-like towers (each costing £1 million) across the straits and to link them with steel boom nets, with the idea of closing the English Channel to enemy ships.

About 3,000 civilian workmen were brought to a quiet backwater at Shoreham and work began on two of these towers: each 40 feet in diameter with latticed steel work surrounding a 90 foot high cylindrical steel tower and built on a hollow 80 foot thick concrete base designed to be flooded and sunk in about 20 fathoms (120 feet) of water. The vast, honeycombed concrete base was shaped with pointed bows and stern for easy towing.

One tower was completed when the war finished in November. The other half-finished giant was broken up for scrap, but it seemed a waste to break up the finished one. After much thought it was decided to use the solitary tower to replace the old Nab Light Vessel by sinking it at the eastern end of the Spithead approaches, thus reducing maintenance and also serving as an invaluable naval defence post, if ever required. It now provides an important navigational aid for ships approaching Portsmouth.

As you walk along here you can see traces of man's various attempts to keep the sea at bay and protect properties atop the crumbling cliffs. There is now a newer sea wall, this may last another 50 years or so but it seems rather a futile effort: the sea will win in the end, it always does. If you are interested in geology, another feature here is the 'raised beach', which is identified by a layer of shingle two-thirds of the way up the cliff, which would have been a beach several thousand years ago, indicating that the sea level was originally much higher than it is now.

At the end of the sea wall is a cluster of little cabins nestling under the cliff, take the path up to the right, by the Long Ledge Café.

Immediately below the café is black Rock Ledge and, to the right, Long Ledge. These, together with Bembridge Ledge continue to be a hazard to the unwary and are the reason why the lifeboat station keeps a RIB in the shed on shore, which can be launched from the beach and used in much shallower water than the larger boat.

At the top of the steps, you should have turned left and continued along the cliff top but a recent fall has meant a temporary diversion which may still be in force, the footpath diversion is clearly indicated. After just under a mile you can return to the cliff path, along BB14. Take care along here as there are frequent cliff falls and in wet weather the clay becomes very slippery; Bembridge Clay is also very sticky stuff and clings to your boots when wet, making them feel like lead weights. After about three-quarters of a mile the path forks, turn left keeping to the cliff path, for a further half a mile.

The path goes past Kingsway Environmental Studies Centre, formerly Bembridge School, easily distinguished by various outdoor activity areas and, usually, hundreds of children.

Just after the school turn right by a board about Bembridge School. There is no sign post at this point but a few yards further on, round the side of a corrugated metal building, you will be able to see a

Bembridge School

Bembridge School was founded in 1919, by social reformer and Liberal MP John Howard Whitehouse, based on the teachings of John Ruskin. It was one of the first schools to incorporate practical subjects like woodwork, long before they became mainstream. The school was noted for its large collection of art, books and memorabilia relating to Ruskin, including many notable manuscripts. The collection is now housed in the Ruskin Library at the University of Lancaster. During the Second World War the site was used as a military base by the Army and the school moved to Brantwood House in Coniston, the former home of John Ruskin, which was owned by the school. The school returned to Bembridge in 1945 but closed in 1997. The premises are now used by Kingsway Environmental Studies Centre.

footpath sign (no number at this end). The path leads into a lane which emerges on Hillway Road. Turn left, walk along the road for about 100 yards then right onto footpath BB22 to Steyne Wood.

Because of the ever-present threat from the French, at the end of the nineteenth century a battery was built in the wood. It was intended for four guns but they never arrived. One reached the Island but got stuck at Steyne Cross, quarter of a mile away, and was eventually sold to the Thorneycroft family; the others never left Portsmouth. Some years later another battery was built on the top of Culver Down, which had the considerable advantage of being higher, overlooking the sea and not needing to fire over land and property, much to the relief of local residents.

Continue along the path for about 400 yards until you reach another road, cross over and go straight on, still on BB22, for a further 100 yards until you reach a junction. Turn right and walk up the track to Bembridge Windmill.

View from the Toll Gate Café across the harbour

Built in the early 18th Century, this is the last surviving windmill on the Island and is now owned by the National Trust.

Passing the windmill brings you to the road to Bembridge. Go straight ahead along this road towards the village for about a third of a mile, until you reach a footpath on your left,BB3 to The Point, next to house number 66. This is a short descent to Brading Marsh Nature Reserve.

When you reach the sign for the reserve turn right; this brings you out in the lane next to the Pilot Boat Inn. If you have waited until the end for your refreshment then round to the left on the harbour edge is the Toll Gate Café.

The Lifeboat View
Open May to September 10am-4pm
Tel: 01983 875568

On the sea wall, this is the cheaper of the two options near the lifeboat station. It is fairly basic, with simple decor, but it is pleasant to sit outside and watch the comings and goings on water and on land. The cakes are freshly made and the tea strong. They have tables inside and out but it is quite small and quickly becomes crowded around lunchtime, so if you want to eat here it is best to book. However they do their best to serve everyone fairly promptly and it isn't usually a problem if you just want drinks and snacks.

They have a good reputation for food and a speciality here is fish, as the proprietor is a fisherman, so lunch menus can vary depending on the morning's catch! They also sell ice-creams and a small array of beach goods.

The Bembridge Coast Hotel
Open all year
Tel: 01983 873931

The other, more expensive, alternative a little further on is the Bembridge Coast Hotel. The staff are very helpful and the place has a pleasant atmosphere. The tea is served in china pots and there is a tempting selection of creamy cakes. You can sit outside on the patio and admire the view, or relax in the lounge and still admire the view.

Being part of the Warner Holidays chain means that menu choices don't change much, so if you go more than once you will probably get the same array of cakes.

Long Ledge Café
Open April to October, 10am-5pm
Not open in very bad weather
Tel: 01983 875120

One of the shacks in this little community has been converted for use as a beach café. It is a family-run business selling teas and coffees, snacks, cakes and burgers along with the usual paraphernalia of buckets and spades, etc. The limited space inside means that tables are outside, on a terrace overlooking Whitecliff Bay. They have sensibly opted for serving tea and coffee in mugs. Service is friendly and efficient.

The Toll Gate Café, Bembridge
Described in walk 4 on page 33.

Long Ledge Café

Walk 7:
Brading

Footpaths and bridleways, some steep, short section on roads. Very varied terrain, chalk downs and marshes, wildlife and local history.

Bull carved out of wood by local artist Paul Sivell

The walk starts from the Bull Ring by the Town Hall, which was used for bull-baiting from the Middle Ages, until 1820 when the practice was outlawed. Its presence in this small town is an indication that Brading was once much more significant than it now is. In fact it had its own Mayor and Town Hall and, in mediaeval times, returned two members to Parliament. It was originally called Ye Kynges Town, having been granted its charter by Edward I in 1282. Note the black bull emerging from a tree stump next to the bus shelter. When the tree there had to be felled, local artist Paul Sivell, who specialises in chainsaw carving, was commissioned to carve a bull out of the remaining stump. He has utilised various dead trees all over the island to create some unusual works of art.

The Walk

From the Bull Ring head west up the Mall, which was formerly the main road, through the older part of the town.

The lower road, to your left, would have been a very marshy area, prone to flooding, until the railway embankment was built and the marsh drained. In fact the sea came to the edge of Brading and the town quay was used from Roman times until 1881.

Distance	5 miles/8km
Start	Bull Ring by the Town Hall
Parking	Pay and display car park in the town or find a place in a side road
Getting there by car	Brading is on the A3055 between Ryde and Sandown
Getting there by bus	Bus number 3 from Ryde and Sandown stops in Brading, ask for the Bull Ring

After about 300 yards turn right up bridleway B39 next to Linden Terrace.

The thatched cottage on the right is known as Little Jane's. Little Jane was a young girl who lived in Brading toward the end of the eighteenth century. She was 'The Young Cottager' in 'Annals of the Poor' written by Revd. Legh Richmond, curate in charge of Brading. In this book he wrote about 'poor and humble folk' who, despite their position, led deeply religious and inspirational lives. She died of consumption at the age of 15 in 1799. The book was very popular and was a source of inspiration to other writers, like Charles Dickens, who is believed to have written David Copperfield whilst staying on the Island.

Keep going straight up the main track for about a mile, turning, as the bible puts, it 'neither to the left nor the right'.

Some of this is ancient woodland with oaks four or five centuries old. Other parts are chalk and have beech and other typical shallow rooted plants such as periwinkles. Over to the right is Nunwell House and its grounds, where Charles II visited Sir William Oglander. Oglander was knighted, and given the house and estate to thank him for services rendered in the Civil War.

At the end of this track are wooden finger posts. Go straight ahead on bridleway B32, which leads you through a metal gate. 50 yards after the gate bear slightly left to reach the top of the downs, where there is a great view. Go through the gate in the corner and continue across the next field to the road. Turn right along the road, taking advantage of the wide verge on this side, for about 600 yards. Then, near the brow of the hill, just after the second lay-by, cross the road and take bridleway B43 down hill to Alverstone.

There are nice views of the south of the Island and it is a good place to see buzzards and kestrels making the most of the lift, generated by the hill, as they search for prey. Often you can see ships out in Sandown Bay; on a slightly hazy day they appear to be floating in mid air.

You are now descending into the Yar Valley. The first part is quite steep. After about 500 yards, look for footpath B45 on the left (at the time of writing there was a stile and a wooden post but the arrow sign had fallen off). Take this path across the field, keeping the hedge on your right. In the bottom corner are two stiles, climb over both then

The old Town Hall, Brading

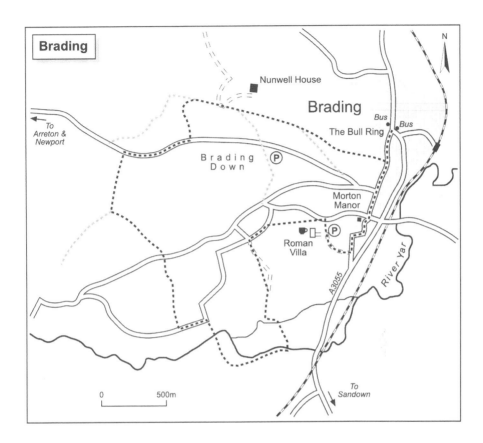

cross the next field diagonally, following the yellow arrow sign, to another stile. Continue in the same direction, towards the houses ahead. Crossing the road you will see footpath B44 going to the left of the house opposite. Follow this path, then after about 200 yards turn right over a stile, across another field and over yet another stile.

Here the path passes through Adgestone vineyard, one of the oldest vineyards in Britain. Local wine producers can take advantage of the warm, south-facing slopes and there is good evidence to suggest that the Romans living at the nearby villa had vineyards in this area.

When you reach the next road turn left, after 200 yards take the footpath, B50, on the right.

You may notice that you are in quite different terrain to the earlier part of the walk. This is flat, marshy ground criss-crossed by small streams. The wildlife is also quite different. Here you may see yellow irises, purple loosestrife and reeds, as well as reed warblers and reed buntings, and herons, standing like sentinels of the waterways.

After 100 yards you will reach a small tributary of the Yar. Once over the small wooden bridge cross the stile at the other end and continue straight ahead, in the direction of the yellow arrow, across the field to the next little, metal-framed bridge. Cross this then, just as you emerge into the field, turn left along the hedge which borders the river.

In summer listen here for the 'zee' of greenfinches and the chiff-chaffs singing their name.

Follow this path along the hedge until you reach some houses, then turn left down some steps and after a few yards turn left again to cross over another footbridge. After bearing slightly to the left to go over a stile, follow the path straight ahead, in the direction of the yellow arrow, to avoid causing too much damage to the plants. It is also the driest route through the boggy areas!

After the next wooden bridge find your way across this marshy area. The path goes just to the left of the bushes in front of you, but you may need to make a few detours to avoid very damp parts. The yellow arrow on the post indicates the general direction but the field is not very big and there is a stile at the other end.

Once over the stile, bear slightly left as the path is in the top left-hand corner of this small field. After the stile turn right for 200 yards to reach the road. Turn right along the road for about 200 yards. On the bend is a footpath off to the right, B47, to the Roman Villa, which is very close although out of sight over the rise. The café is in the Roman Villa. To reach it go straight ahead, to the left of the building. Just before the path meets the road, turn right onto footpath B48, the gate to Brading Roman Villa is just along here.

It is worth stopping by the gates and looking around. The villa's lands extended to the coast and encompassed a large and prosperous farm. The incline you are on meant that the villa was safe from flooding, the sea came much further inland than it now does, in winter parts of this walk would have been under water.

This is one of only two surviving villas on the island, and is one of the best preserved in Europe, largely thanks to the decline of Brading as a settlement. The remains that have lain undisturbed under farm land for all these centuries, would probably have been damaged or obliterated under urban sprawl had the town expanded.

When you have finished your refreshment, turn right out of the gate and go down the drive to Morton Old Road and turn left. After 300 yards turn left again onto Morton Manor Road. This emerges on Hornsey Rise, which leads to the other end of The Mall. Crossing over and following the road round to the left will bring you back to where you started, with only a short section of heavy traffic.

The Forum Café, Brading Roman Villa

The Villa is open every day from 10am-5pm but the café is only open until 4pm.
Tel: 01983 406223

The modern design gives a light, airy feel and provides lovely views on both sides. There are also some tables outside. There is a tempting array of cakes and snacks which are made in the kitchens here, the sandwiches and baguettes are freshly made to order and they do particularly delicious brownies. Tea is served in proper china teapots, which is always nice, and they serve good quality coffee. It is also licensed and serves a small selection of wine and the local

Plaque in the café

Goddards Ale. The café also hosts historical and archaeological lectures and there are always children's activities in the foyer.

Walk 8:
Arreton Vale and Newchurch

Gentle walk through farm land on footpaths and bridleways.

Distance	7 miles/11km
Start	School Lane, next to Arreton Primary School
Parking	There is parking at Arreton Old Village or next to the White Lion pub (outside school hours only)
Getting there by car	Arreton is on the A 3056 between Newport and Sandown
Getting there by bus	Number 8 from Newport and Sandown, ask for Arreton School

The path begins next to Arreton Primary School which, if you parked at Arreton Old Village, is a little further along the road past the White Lion. The path, School Lane, is signed bridleway A9 to Mersley, and carries pretty much straight on in the same general direction, apart from a few little wiggles round the edges of a fieldfields and one 50 yard dog-leg where the path crosses a bridleway, for about one and a half miles until you reach a road. The only major difficulty is working out which side of the hedge to be on, generally one side has a better worn path than the other but, as it is arable land, there are no gates for cattle so it isn't too much of a problem as long as you avoid damaging crops.

This walk is quite different to the others in this book. There are no downs to climb and the River Yar, rather than the sea for water interest, it is altogether a softer, gentler sort of walk. As you walk this first part, over to the right are the long greenhouses of Wight Salads,

St George's, Arreton

who are major salad vegetable suppliers, so you may well have eaten some of their produce.

When you reach the road, turn left and walk 50 yards to a track, next to a house, signposted footpath NC1 to Mersley and Knighton. After 50 yards the path curves round to the right, now signposted NC7. Follow this path as it winds its way to the next road. Here, turn right and walk about 50 yards to the bend in the road, then carry straight on down the dead-end road ahead, byway NC45a to Lower Knighton. After 200 yards, ignore the next bend in the road and go straight ahead, down bridleway NC53, towards the cycleway.

At the cycleway turn left and walk along here for about three-quarters of a mile. This is an old railway line and about 300 yards after a somewhat dilapidated railway bridge over the Yar, is a crossroad. Turn right here onto NC11 to Newchurch and go over a wooden bridge. Once through the kissing gate walk up the slope and through another gate,

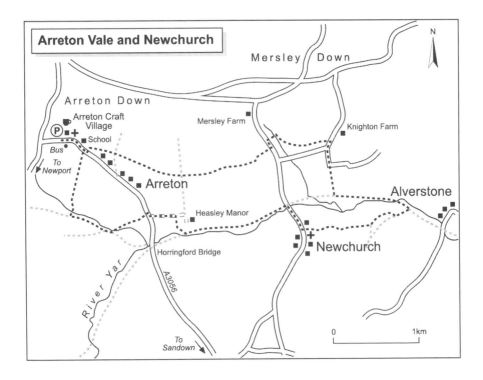

then turn right. Follow this path through Youngwoods Copse for about half a mile until you reach a gate, marked with yellow arrows, onto a T-junction. Turn right here and cross a plank bridge into a newly planted woodland area recently created by the Forestry Commission.

Keeping to the right, head through here until you reach the village of Newchurch, whose pretty, white-towered church was visible for much of the early part of the walk.

The church was originally built by a cousin of William the Conqueror to whom the Isle of Wight had been given.

When you reach the main road, turn right. Just after the bridge turn left to rejoin the cycleway. A stroll along here of about three-quarters of a mile will take you to Haseley Manor which is easily visible from the path.

The present owners have created new wildlife ponds here. These were still in their infancy when I passed, so hopefully they have become home to some interesting flora and fauna. Sometimes there are things that look like badminton nets set up by the ponds. These are actually for trapping birds so that they can be ringed and their movements tracked.

Just after the first pond, take the footpath A14, which is clearly indicated, to your right, to the Manor, then turn left along Heasley Lane (they weren't very consistent with spellings round here). This leads you to the main road, the A3056.

You can walk back along this road, Arreton Old Village is about a mile to the right, but a more pleasant route is to take footpath A1 on the other side of the road, just to your right. Go up here through a garden, over a gate and straight across the field to a stile. Continue straight ahead. At the next path junction go straight ahead. Follow the path for 200 yards until you can see a plank bridge on your left, which you

Haseley Manor

Haseley Manor

Haseley Manor has been inhabited almost continuously for 1,000 years. It is known to have belonged to King Harold, prior to the Battle of Hastings. On his death his property was claimed by his conqueror and the Domesday Book of 1086 describes it as belonging to William the Conqueror. The house was passed down to his son Henry I who later gifted it to his steward Humprey de Bohun. Then, in 1136, the de Bohun family sold it to the monks of Quarr Abbey who farmed the lands for the next 400 years until the dissolution of the abbey under Henry VIII.

The manor passed through various hands after this until it was bought in 1976 by the Young family, with whom it remains.

need to cross. After this little bridge walk up the path to the metal gate to the right. Go through the gate and straight ahead with the fence on your left and the stream on your right. After 100 yards there is another gate, then a little copse.

After the copse turn immediately right. Walk along the field edge, cross the bridge and stile then bear slightly left, following the direction of the yellow arrow, to the following stile, which is out of sight at the top of the hill. From here head straight across the field to the houses in front of you. These fields are often filled with the sound of larks and linnets. When you reach the road, turn left. Turn right by the White Lion up footpath A12 and enter Arreton Old Village either through Lavender and Lace shop or through St George's churchyard, and past the carp pond (mentioned in the Domesday Book) where you will find The Dairyman's Daughter.

The Dairyman's Daughter gets its name from a book about a young woman called Elizabeth Wallbridge, who was born in 1770. The Vicar of Brading, the Reverend Legh Richmond, chronicled her life, conversion to Methodism and death of consumption at the age of 30. The book influenced writers from Charlotte Bronte to Charles Dickens and was the most widely read religious tract of the 19th century. Her grave in the church at Arreton was a scene of pilgrimage for thousands, including Queen Victoria.

The Dairyman's Daughter, Arreton Old Village
Open all year
Tel: 01983 539361

The Dairyman's Daughter is a pub and tea rooms, in the centre of the craft village, with oak beams and various antiques and curios to look at. The place also houses a museum of rural life. The courtyard outside the tea rooms is surrounded with various agricultural artefacts, which gives you something to look at as you relax with your cuppa. The tea and coffee is good and the cakes obviously fresh. The cream teas are generously sized with two kinds of jam and lovely thick, yellow clotted cream. The service is friendly and helpful.

If you want something more substantial, the food tends to be fairly standard pub fare although they do sometimes have interesting specials; the meals arrive fairly promptly and are good value.

Walk 9:
Godshill and Appuldurcombe

Great views and a historic house. On footpaths and bridleways,
some parts very steep.

Distance	5 miles/8km
Start	Car park in Godshill
Parking	Large free car park in Godshill village
Getting there by car	Godshill straddles the A3020
Getting there by bus	Buses 2 and 3 from Newport, get off in the village centre by the Griffin pub

On leaving the car park, cross the road and go up the Hollow Lane opposite. The footpath, GL57, is on your left, running behind the Griffin pub gardens.

At the end of the pub garden hedge the path emerges in a field. Keep to the right here along the field boundary. Go through the kissing gate at the other end of the field into a copse – be careful as it is easy to lose the path in the copse. One path goes to the right after the gate, crosses a plank bridge then climbs up though the wood to a small gate; the other way is to go straight ahead after the kissing gate and follow a small path up to a larger track, turning right along here for 100 yards to arrive at the same small gate.

Go through the gate. Walking along here you will pass Sainham Farm on your right. Immediately after the farm, turn left and take the Worsley Trail GL58 to Gatcliff, a little chert outcrop on the north end of chalk downs, surmounted by the Worsley Monument.

The Worsleys were major landowners from the 15th to the 19th century. Sir Richard, Governor of the Isle of Wight, wrote a history of

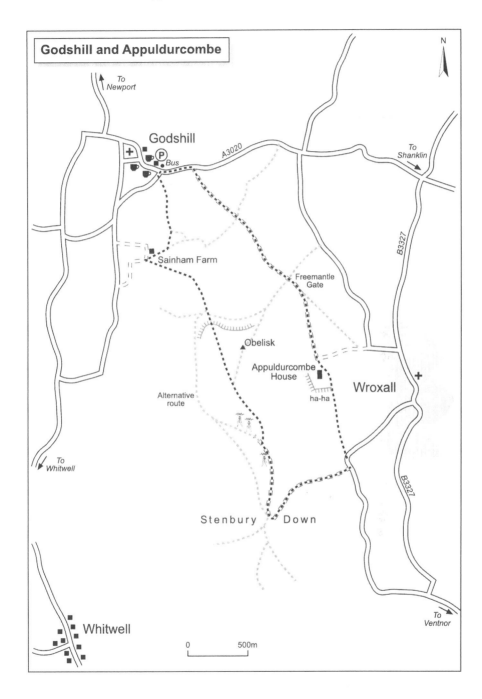

Godshill and Appuldurcombe

the Island that is still considered to be a definitive work on the subject today. They also built Appuldurcombe House (see below).

As you walk up here, almost at once the views to the left open up and you should be able to see a white, truncated obelisk on top of Ashey Down, erected in 1735 by Trinity House as a sea-mark. A little further, on the right, you will begin to see the cliffs at the western end of the Island.

The trail passes through several sets of very high farm gates set in unusually high fences – there used to be an ostrich farm here. Finally you will reach a path junction with a sign post. There are two alternatives at this point depending on how fit you are feeling. You can either go straight ahead, continuing on GL58, up the steps onto Gatcliff itself. This is very steep and there are about 200 steps, but the view is well worth the effort, or turn right right along GL49 and

Appuldurcombe House

When Sir James Worsley married Anne Leigh he acquired the considerable Leigh estates, including Appuldurcombe. He was a former page and whipping boy for the future Henry VIII. Henry later visited Sir James here and probably hunted in the surrounding woods. The present house was begun in 1702 and extended by Sir Richard Worsley who also had the grounds designed by Capability Brown. As you approach you will see the ha-ha, the ditch that separated the garden from the park, that Brown was so fond of including. The estate was sold off in 1855 after which the house had a variety of occupants, including the monks of Solesmes who had been forced into exile from France. They later moved a little further north to Quarr Abbey. Service men were billeted here in the war until 1943, when a Dornier Do 217 engaged on a mine laying mission turned inland and dropped its final mine very close to the house, before crashing into St Martin's Down. For many years it lay derelict before being taken over by a trust who began its restoration. It now belongs to English Heritage, who have found creative ways to use the site, including staging open air plays and concerts with the house as a back drop. It is open to the public from April to October.

Appuldurcombe House

follow the bridleway round the edge, bearing left at each junction, following the old estate boundary wall.

If you go up Gatcliff, from the top, on a clear day, you can see as far as Selsey Bill to the east and St Alban's head to the West. Looking to the north-east you may also be able to make out the Nab Tower lighthouse. This light is responsible for guiding ships into the deep water channel for Portsmouth and Southampton. There is a footpath off to the left to the Worsley monument, if you want to make the detour.

The two paths meet up again near the masts, at the point where they join the station's metalled track. Follow this track past a second communications mast for about 600 yards. The hedges here are dotted with gorse.

Gorse is a native plant with a distinctive coconut scent, that although flowering most abundantly in Spring, has some flowers on it all year round, hence the old country saying, "When the gorse is out of bloom kissing is out of fashion".

You can now see the resort of Ventnor in front of you. Continue following the metalled track, round to the left as it goes down hill for about half a mile, past some disused pits, to a small lane (Rew Lane), and turn left. After 100 yards leave the road and follow the footpath GL47 straight ahead. The footpath goes to the right of the farm yard and continues across the fields for about half a mile to the beautiful Appuldurcombe House.

The footpath now follows the iron railings, then a short section of stone wall, to the entrance of the grounds marked by a stone gate house, also the location of the Isle of Wight Owl and Falconry Centre.

Godshill

Godshill itself is a charming village with lots of pretty, thatched cottages. The village gets its name from the strange story surrounding the building of the church. It is said that originally the church was to be built in the centre of the village and the builders began in the chosen location. They stopped work for the night but when they returned the next morning they found that everything had been moved to the top of the hill. Thinking it was some sort of practical joke, they carried everything back down and continued building. The next night the same thing happened, and the next night. The builders of the church wanted to discover who was moving the stones and posted two guards to watch during the night. While keeping vigil they were astonished to see angels moving the stones up the hill.

This was taken to be a sign from God that the church should be built on the top of the hill, and so the site was named Godshill. The church contains monuments to the Worsley family and the tomb of Sir John Leigh, former owner of Appuldurcombe House, and is among the top 10 most visited churches in the UK. The village itself is host to many attractions including the Model Village, which depicts the entire area in miniature, and The Old Smithy, a former blacksmiths forge, which is now a gift shop and fashion boutique.

A small part of the large estate, which once surrounded the house, is still intact, with other features of the estate still visible in the surrounding farmland. Occasionally you may see birds of prey being exercised in the fields near to the Wight Owl and Falconry Centre.

Cross the road and follow the footpath opposite for another half mile, which leads to the original entrance to the park, the Freemantle Gate. These gates rather ingeniously incorporate an early self-closing mechanism that still allows the gate to open both ways. Once through the gate, go straight ahead and follow this bridle path to the main road. Along the way you will pass Godshill Park Farm which, as well as being a livery stables, also houses llamas. Once you reach the road, Godshill village is about 200 yards to your left.

The Old World Tea Rooms, Godshill
Open all year 10am-5pm
Tel: 01983 840637

There are several tea shops in Godshill, but my one of my favourites is the Old World Tea Rooms opposite the car park. These tea rooms are housed in a 17th Century thatched cottage. If you can, sit outside in the garden as the low roofed extension has a rather claustrophobic and depressing feel which belies the excellence of the cream teas and the freshness of the homemade cakes. The place has a very relaxed and unpretentious atmosphere with tea served in metal teapots.

The service is excellent, being friendly and helpful – I have been served very late in the day, in the off season, by smiling, welcoming staff who, if they did want to get off home, certainly didn't show it!

The Willow Tree Tea Gardens
Open April to October 10am-5pm
Tel: 01983 840633

If you enjoy gardening then you may like to try The Willow Tree, which is at the other end of the High Street, opposite the Model Village. They serve a perfectly respectable cream tea, which you can sit and eat amidst the rather impressive topiary. I can't even begin to imagine how much effort it must take to maintain this.

The Hollies Tea Rooms
Open February to November, 10am-5pm
Tel: 01983 840223

The entrance to the Hollies is marked by a rather grand set of iron
gates leading to pretty gardens, or you can sit inside in the vinery,
which dates from 1850, with, in summer, bunches of grapes dangling
above your head. There is always a good array of cakes on display, all
homemade, and they often do 'cake of the day' special offers. They
also do light lunches and Minghella's Ice Cream, which is made here
on the Island. In fact the owners try to use local produce in their food
as much as possible.
The service is very friendly and efficient and they will give you a top
up of hot water or milk if you want it.

Other teashops in the village are The Batswing, The Old Smithy and
Chocolate Island.

Thatched cottages in Church Hill with All Saints church behind

Walk 10:
Bonchurch and Luccombe

Steep footpaths, very picturesque. One very narrow cleft of rock.

Distance	4½ or 5½ miles/7 or 9 km
Start	The top of Bonchurch Shute
Parking	There is plenty of parking on the A3055, near the top of Bonchurch Shute and in the little parking area just to the south
Getting there by car	Bonchurch lies just off the A3055 between Sandown and Ventnor
Getting there by bus	Buses number 3 and 16 between Ventnor and Shanklin. Get off at the top of Bonchurch Shute

The walk begins at the top of Bonchurch Shute, which is sign-posted to Bonchurch Village. Head down to the first right-hand bend in the road. Take footpath V66 here on the left, which quickly descends through the lush woodlands of The Landslip to the Coastal Path. Turn left when you reach this lower path.

This is a very popular place to walk with lots of digressions to viewpoints along the way.

Keep to the main Coastal Path, following the blue signs, which is well-maintained with steps and handrails in the steepest parts. After about three-quarters of a mile the path emerges from The Landslip through a wooden gate onto a small road. Turn left along here for about 200 yards then bear right along an avenue of chestnuts, which descends into Luccombe Chine. At the bottom of the dip there is a path down to the beach, but the walk continues straight on, following the signs to Luccombe (signposts but no path numbers).

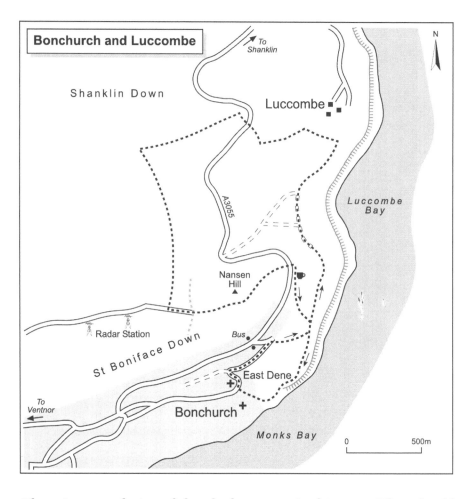

There is an profusion of thatched cottages in this area. What should the collective noun be, can you have a sheaf of cottages? Or maybe a bale?

Due to the shelter from the downs to the north, the climate in this area is particularly mild, hence the Mediterranean appearance of many gardens. There is an abundance of palms and other exotic plants, and even the odd fruiting olive tree. Holm oaks do very well here and grow wild in The Landslip, I wonder if anyone has started truffle-hunting there yet?

In Luccombe village there is a signpost, usually with a table of jams and chutneys under it, turn left here towards Luccombe Farm onto footpath SS88. Go up the road for about 100 yards then, as the road goes to the right, take the footpath straight ahead (still SS88). This leads onto a drive. At the top of the drive turn left to follow the footpath along the hedge. When you reach a gate and path junction turn right, onto SS5, and walk up the field to the main road. Cross the road and go up the bridleway SS9a, signposted to Luccombe Down. After 50 yards turn sharp left to continue on the bridleway (otherwise you will be back on the road again). When you reach the top, turn left at the signpost onto bridleway V43, towards Wroxall Down.

There are fantastic views right across the island and to the mainland beyond, so it is a good place to stop and catch your breath. Dickens was apparently particularly taken with these downs, when he rented a house in Bonchurch in the summer of 1845. The chalk downs are a good spot to see butterflies like the Common Blue and the Chalkhill Blue. If you are very lucky you may see the rare Dartford Warbler, a bird which is fond of this type of gorse scrub.

Looking across Luccombe Chine

It is a pleasant stroll of just over half a mile, along the top, to the radio station where you need to turn left along the perimeter fence.

There are burial mounds to your left here. It was common practice to bury Bronze Age chiefs up on the heights, but it must have been an awful lot of effort to cart everything up here.

Just past the end of the fence there is a signpost: take footpath V123 to Nansen Hill (down to the left).

It is said it is possible to see France from here, I personally never have, but on a clear day you can certainly see to the east, as far as Selsey Bill.

Follow the path on down over a stile and towards the road. Cross the road to the little car park. In the car park take the path off to the right.

Bear to the right and where the path forks take the right hand branch to stay on the upper level, which leads into the Smuggler's Haven Tea Gardens, a mere 100 yards from the car park.

When you have finished your refreshment, either go back to the road and turn left to return to the starting point, or use the footpath at the bottom of the gardens turning right to descend the Devil's Chimney, a narrow cleft in the limestone rock. At the bottom of the cleft turn right and continue down the steps; there are quite a lot of them but there are handrails to help. When you reach the signpost at the bottom, turn right.

Originally a path went across higher up but as you walk back you will be able to see that this is not

Path through The Landslip   *called The Landslip for nothing.*

The Landslip, Bonchurch

The Landslip, as it is today, was created by two major landslides in 1810 and 1818, and a third in 1928. These were due to very heavy rainfall causing the gravel and chalk layers to become heavy and exerting excessive pressure on the Gault clay resulting in slippage. Gault clay is known locally as Blue Slipper, due to its blue-grey colour, and the fact that it becomes very slippery in wet weather. (Blue Slipper on a beach is soft enough to lose your boot in!) Small slippages still occur from time to time, making it unsuitable for building on. Bits of footpath disappear regularly and, in more recent years, parts of the road have been damaged. After the ground has had time to settle again new paths can be created through The Landslip. The warmth and dampness of the area means that the vegetation is lush, providing a very popular amenity.

A little further on, you will see steps and a sign to Bonchurch Shute, carry on past here following the Coastal Path until you leave The Landslip, once again by a wooden gate. The path takes you past some houses, originally built for the staff of East Dene, but now used as holiday cottages, and the estate wall.

At the end of the stone wall there is a path that continues on to Monks Bay, which is quite a pleasant place to swim, although the walk follows the Coastal Path turning right through a gap in the wall to follow the cliff edge. About 200 yards on the path forks. Take the right hand branch towards the chimneys of a large house, which is East Dene.

The poet Swinburne lived at East Dene and is one of numerous literary figures connected with this part of the island.

The path emerges on a tiny road by Old St Boniface Church, which dates back to 1070 but was probably built on the site of an earlier Anglo-Saxon church.

The Island is reputed to have been the last place in England to accept Christianity and St Boniface was the priest who brought it here.

From the old church walk up hill past the gates of East Dene, following the road round to the left, then at the junction turn right. This is Bonchurch Shute, and following this as it curves upwards, out of Bonchurch, takes you back to the start of the walk.

The Smuggler's Haven Tea Gardens, Upper Bonchurch
Open 10am-4.30pm in summer and at Easter
Tel: 01983 852992

There is a small, cosy seating area inside the cabin and plenty of tables outside, set in a lovely vantage point with views across the top of The Landslip to the sea; a relaxing way to enjoy a well earned cup of tea. They serve fresh homemade cakes and other simple fare. The owners generate a kindly atmosphere and will happily provide an extra teabag if you like strong tea, or a top-up with hot water if you don't.

Smuggler's Haven Tea Gardens

Walk 11:
St Lawrence and the Botanic Gardens

Coastal walk, great views, some parts very steep. Along part of the pilgrim paths. Some along main road.

Distance	5½ miles/9km
Start	Botanic Gardens car park
Parking	The Botanic Gardens has a large pay and display car park
Getting there by car	Ventnor Botanic Gardens are on the A3055 just to the west of Ventnor
Getting there by bus	Buses numbers 6 and 16 from Ventnor stop just outside the gates

From the car park make your way across the gardens to the cliff path. When you reach the cliff, turn right to head towards the south of the Island along the coastal footpath, which is marked at intervals with the blue Coastal Path signs.

There are great sea views along here, and even from the cliff top you can hear the sea crashing onto the rocks below, and it is possible to get down to the beach at several points. These small, secluded coves, hardly visible from any other part of the coast, made this ideal smugglers' territory, although the surrounding rocks must have made it quite a risky venture.

About a mile along here, at Woody Bay, the path turns right to skirt some cottages. When you reach the tarmac turn left over a stile then, after 50 yards, turn left again following the yellow arrow, to rejoin the cliff path on the other side of the cottages. There is a path to the left here giving access to the Bay itself, which is an SSSI, if you want a swim. Otherwise the walk continues over the stile, round the copse and back to the cliff edge.

As with many other coastal areas of the Island, you can still see evidence of WWII defences in the fields. During the war much of the coast was forbidden to civilians, so walks like this would not have been possible.

Just beyond here you get a sight of St Catherine's Lighthouse. You may wonder why it isn't higher. It was originally, as you will see later in the walk, but sea mists are so common here that it was often shrouded. Its present position puts it below most sea frets and the main light, visible for up to 30 nautical miles in clear weather, is the third most powerful light in the Trinity House Service.

After a further three-quarters of a mile you will reach a small stream and some wooden steps which lead into Old Park, go up these and follow the path ahead, then after 200 yards turn left to stay in the woods. There are numerous winding paths through this woodland but as long as you stick to fairly well used paths, and keep going up hill, you will eventually reach the road.

It used to be possible to walk through the Undercliff to St Catherine's but, unfortunately, due to cliff falls, the path is not accessible at present although this may change as the ground settles. When you reach the road turn left. Just over half a mile along here you will see a signpost for footpath NT117, to the Cripple Path, on your right. Be careful because this path is very steep but it is a great place to see cliff loving birds.

In spring and summer you can see martins and swallows nesting in the overhanging ledges.

Ledges on the cliff make great nesting places for Hirundines

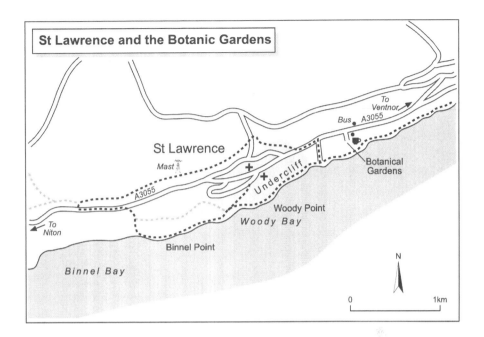

When you reach the top, turn right onto Coastal Footpath NT28 to Ventnor to begin the return leg, 100 metres higher than the outward one, according to the ordnance survey map. After about half a mile you will reach the highest point of the walk. Behind you is St Catherine's lighthouse again, and further inland the remains of the two older ones on top of St Catherine's Hill.

From the top you can see, nestled between the hills, the village of Whitwell, the site of a holy well or 'White Well', said to have healing powers. The path you are walking on is one of the 'pilgrim paths' to Whitwell, hence the name 'Cripple Path'.

A little further you will cross another pilgrim way, St Rhadegund's path, leading to the village itself. However, this walk continues straight ahead for half a mile on the cliff top to St Lawrence Shute, now following footpath V77.

When you reach St Lawrence Shute go down the steps to the road. Cross the road, go up the steps on the other side and turn right towards St Lawrence. About 300 yards further on there is a steep path down to your right V76. Go down here following the handrails. At the bottom of the cliff follow the well-used path into a small wood continuing in a downwards direction until you reach the main road.

Turn left along the road and walk along until you find footpath V91, on the right about 100 yards after the wood, to Ventnor Botanic Gardens, which are on the left at the bottom of this path.

Royal Gardens Café, Ventnor Botanic Gardens
Tel. 01983 855570

These gardens have been estab-lished in the grounds of the old TB hospital and are interesting at anytime of the year. They are popular with young and old alike. The place is wheel chair friendly with slopes everywhere and a lift down to the café. There is also a children's play area. The café is in the lowest part of the building, by the pond. Above it is an exhibition centre and, as well as a permanent display, there

The Royal Gardens Café at Ventnor Botanic Gardens

St Catherine's Lighthouse

The earliest of the lighthouses here was built, in 1330, by Walter de Godeton as an act of penance for plundering wine from the wreck of St Marie of Bayonne in Chale Bay. He was fined 287 marks for the theft by the courts, but the Church threatened to excommunicate him unless he built the lighthouse as well. He also paid for a priest to maintain a light there and to say mass each day for the souls of those lost at sea. The tower is known locally as the 'Pepper Pot' and is the only surviving mediaeval lighthouse. Next to it is the stump of another lighthouse, begun in 1785, but never completed, now known as the 'salt cellar'. The newest one was built in 1837, after 'The Clarendon' was wrecked on the rocks below. Down there it is below the many sea-mists that often shrouded the lights higher up.

are often art shows and presentations focusing particularly on plants. The café is fairly large as it is very popular and is nearly always busy. The tea comes in good sized china pots with matching crockery. The cakes are homemade and include interesting things such as hazelnut meringues served with cream. If you want something savoury the soup is always good and they do nice, wholesome snacks. They pride themselves on being non-GM and mostly organic. There are tables inside or benches out on the terrace, which is a real sun-trap and usually warm enough to be pleasant until quite late in the year.

Ventnor Botanic Gardens

Walk 12:
Carisbrooke and Gatcombe

Footpaths and bridleways, steep in parts. Good views of the Island, good wildlife walk.

Distance	4½ miles/7km
Start	Car park in Whitcombe Road
Parking	Car park in Whitcombe Road which is behind Carisbrooke Castle and opposite the Carisbrooke Priory
Getting there by car	Take the Whitcombe road on the south-east side of Newport
Getting there by bus	Bus numbers 6 and 36 from Newport, get off at the Priory

Head off to the west from the car park along the path by the road, which gives you a lovely view of Carisbrooke Castle and the valley below. It is easy to see why it was such a good site to build a castle. At the corner of Froglands Lane take the public bridleway N108 to Gatcombe.

This shady, tree-lined path, known locally as Dark Lane, opens out to fine panoramic views of the Island. It is a good place to hear linnets and larks and to watch buzzards as they soar across the fields searching for food.

Continue along this path for just under a mile until you reach a wooden signpost, then veer left to Gatcombe on bridleway G6. Continue straight on for another half mile.

To your left, the River Medina has cut through the chalk ridge that runs like a spine across the Isle of Wight.

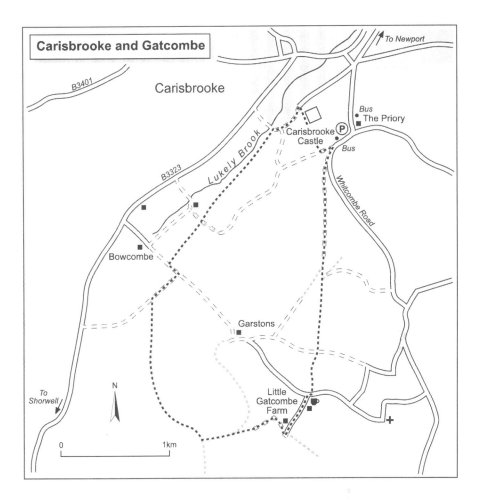

Down in the river valley is the tall brick tower of Whitecroft, once the local mental hospital, in the days when it was thought better to isolate such people from the community. Now it is a location for the local NHS trust, and also used by the Education Authority. In the distance, if it is clear, you can see Culver Down, the cliffs at the Eastern end of the Island's chalk ridge known as the backbone of the Isle of Wight.

You can also see evidence of badger setts along here, although seeing the badgers themselves is trickier as they are notoriously shy, mostly emerging at dusk to feed.

Carisbrooke Castle from the car park at the start of the walk

When you reach the crossroads, continue straight ahead on path G6, down the hill to Little Gatcombe. Turn right when you reach the road, and in 10 yards you will see a sign for Little Gatcombe Farm B&B and teagardens, in Newbarn Lane.

When you have finished your refreshment, continue your walk along Newbarn Lane for about 500 yards. Follow the lane as it curves around to the right then left past Newbarn Farm. After the farm, the track becomes a path and takes a sharp turn to the left, which is not signposted, and you start to rise again over the smooth undulations of Dukem Down. As you near the top you should be able to catch a glimpse of the sea behind you. Watch here for the signpost to a short, steep path on the right, bridleway G22. At the top of this short path (50 yards) turn left towards Dukem Copse, still path G22, and continue climbing the down.

As you reach the highest point of the walk you should be able to see the Pepper Pot on St Catherine's Down to the south, and to the north the

Spinnaker tower in Portsmouth. As you walk, the west of the Isle of Wight begins to open up, giving views of most of the Island.

When you reach the copse, go through a gate then turn right and follow the bridle path N146 to Bowcombe. After quarter of a mile, the path leaves the copse. Keep going straight ahead along the field edges towards another copse, keeping the fence on your right. At the bottom of this field is a gate into Froglands Copse. This next little bit is steep and can be very muddy, but it is short! As you emerge from this into a field you will be able to see the castle in front of you.

In the field, bear left round the edge of the field, then right onto the track at the bottom. Turn left, after 400 yards, onto another track. 50 yards along you should be able to see a footpath on your right marked with a blue arrow, making the division between two fields.

At high summer this is a wonderful place to hear skylarks, although for how much longer, with changing farming methods is anyone's guess.

At the end of this path is Froglands Lane, turn left into the lane for a few yards and look for footpath N104, to Clatterford, on your right. This path will take you past Plaish Farm and along the side of Lukely Brook, a pretty area with yellow flags growing in the marshy ground in summer. This brings you out in Clatterford Shute, by a ford. Turn right into the road then, after a few yards take N88 to Carisbrooke Castle, on your left. At the top of this path cross the car park and take the wooden gate on your right, leaving the castle on your left. At the corner of the castle take the path on your right marked by yellow arrows. Follow this path across the valley and into Froglands Lane, turn left to Whitcombe Road and the car park.

Parasol mushrooms

Opposite the car park is Carisbrooke Priory. This was

Carisbrooke Castle

Carisbrooke Castle is famous as the last place of imprisonment of Charles I before he was taken back to London to be executed. He also held his last parliament in Newport in a last-ditch attempt to reach a compromise with his lords, although it turned out that Charles wasn't too good at compromise! What is less well known is that, as was the custom in those days, his family were held captive here too. During his imprisonment his daughter Elizabeth became ill and died in the Castle. She is buried at St Thomas Church in Newport, and is the only member of the Royal family to be buried in an ordinary Parish church.

---

formerly a convent, but is now a Christian Centre for prayer and healing open to anyone Monday to Friday 10 am to 4pm and also serves tea and coffee Tuesday to Friday between 10 am and 12:00 noon.

The Gatcombe Tea Rooms, Little Gatcombe Farm, Newbarn Lane

Open all year 12noon-5pm
Tel: 01983 721580

The tea rooms occupy the conservatory and garden. If you arrive at a slack time you may have to call to get someone to serve you. The place is very clean and they have a good selection of cakes, although outside peak times the homemade scones may not be very fresh. Rather unusually, you are given a pot of hot water and choose a teabag yourself from a wide selection of teas and tisanes to make your own tea in your cup, which will probably suit those who don't like their tea too strong.

You can sit inside in the conservatory or at tables outside, although being in a valley, there are no great panoramas to be enjoyed.

This is probably not the best tea room on the Island but it has the advantage of being the only one in this area, and there are lots of lovely walks and cycle rides from here.

Walk 13:
Compton

Footpaths on downs and cliff-tops, great views, some steep.

Distance	5½ miles/9km
Start	National Trust Car Park at Compton Bay
Parking	National Trust Car Park at Compton Bay
Getting there by car	Bay is on the A3055 just south of Freshwater
Getting there by bus	Bus number 12 from Freshwater, ask for Compton Bay

From the car park head inland along the track, which is sign posted F55, towards Compton Farm. The path goes to the right of the farm buildings, over a stile, and is clearly marked. Follow the path uphill and through a gate, then continue along the top of the ridge for about three-quarters of a mile.

From here are good views ahead to the south of the island and immediately ahead is Brook Hill House, once the home of the author JB Priestly, one of many literary figures who have fallen in love with the Isle of Wight. On your right, out to sea is Hanover point, which is famous for its Dinosaur footprints and fossil forest. Next to it is Compton Beach, which is popular with surfers because of the long fetch (the distance a wave is able to travel before it reaches the shore) coming in from the North Atlantic.

Continue following the path through various gates, until it emerges in a farm track. Keep going in the same general direction for about half a mile, until you reach a wide chalk track, on your left, with signs banning cars and motorbikes for part of the year – necessary because

Compton Farm

Footpaths on downs and cliff-tops, great views, some steep.

From the car park head inland along the track, which is sign posted F55, towards Compton Farm. The path goes to the right of the farm buildings, over a stile, and is clearly marked. Follow the path uphill and through a gate, then continue along the top of the ridge for about three-quarters of a mile.

From here are good views ahead to the south of the island and immediately ahead is Brook Hill House, once the home of the author JB Priestly, one of many literary figures who have fallen in love with the Isle of Wight. On your right, out to sea is Hanover point, which is famous for its Dinosaur footprints and fossil forest. Next to it is Compton Beach, which is popular with surfers because of the long fetch (the distance a wave is able to travel before it reaches the shore) coming in from the North Atlantic.

Freshwater Bay – this rock is known as the Stag

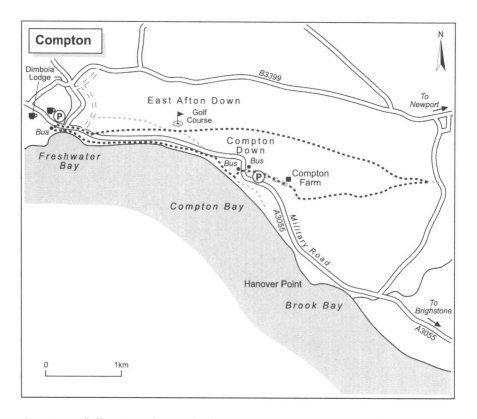

Continue following the path through various gates, until it emerges in a farm track. Keep going in the same general direction for about half a mile, until you reach a wide chalk track, on your left, with signs banning cars and motorbikes for part of the year – necessary because this track is in fact part of the ancient highway from Carisbrooke, now designated byway S26.

Highways are very difficult to close permanently when they are in use and require applications to the Government, but the increase in numbers of quad-bikes and other off road vehicles, in this very popular walking area, necessitated some sort of action.

Turn left onto this byway and head up hill to the top of Brook Down, where there are great views of Tennyson Down and the west of the Island.

The antiquity of this route is attested to by the burial mounds along the route, which date back to at least the Bronze Age. The steepness of the slopes, to your left, make it popular for kestrels and paragliders alike. The openness and the short grass also make it a good place to see wheatears and linnets.

Continue along this clearly defined path for just over a mile, where the path goes through a gate into Freshwater Golf Course. Carry on through here down towards Freshwater Bay, following the old Highway, F33. When you reach the road turn right down into the bay itself, where you will find the Freshwater Bay Tea Rooms next to the car park. An alternative is Cameron Tea Rooms in Dimbola Lodge, a little further on past the public toilets (described in walk 14).

From the car park cross the road to the beach and turn left along the promenade, past Freshwater Lifeboat station. Go up the steps at the end and follow the Coastal Path along the cliff-top.

The cliffs here are either chalk or sandstone, both of which are very prone to erosion, something that is very obvious when you look back along the old road. Look out along here for chalkland butterflies such as the small blue and the chalkhill blue. Also, in spring and early summer, dotted along the cliff, are bright clumps of thrift or sea pink and edible sea kale.

After about three-quarters of a mile the path climbs up to the road for a short distance. Once over the rise, it is worth taking footpath F35, off to the right, to avoid the road and cut the corner off. Once over the footbridge, bear left towards the gate and signpost, where the walk ends, back at the car park.

Freshwater Bay Tea Rooms
Open April to October, 10am-5pm

Despite being in the centre of the bay, and no more than 50 yards away, you can't actually see the sea from these tea rooms. The café gardens are low lying and very close to the Marsh, so it is necessary to have a sea wall to protect the area from flooding. Even so it is probable that eventually the sea will breach the defences and leave the western end of the Island cut off. Meanwhile the tea rooms continue to enjoy their good location.

They serve good tea, plus a pot of hot water, with generously sized home-made cakes in a mish-mash of crockery, as well as ice-cream and pre-packed sandwiches and baguettes to take away. Light lunches eaten on the premises are attractively presented and the place is generally good value for money.

Walk 14:
Mottistone Down

Great views to north and west. Steep in places. Footpaths, byways, and minor roads, steep in places. The first part is suitable for all terrain buggies.

Distance	5 miles/8km
Start	Mottistone Down National Trust car park
Parking	Park in Mottistone Down National Trust car park on Lynch Lane
Getting there by car	Lynch Lane runs from Brighstone in the south to the Sun Inn on the B3401 from Newport
Getting there by bus	Bus number 12 to Mottistone, walk up to the Longstone and begin the walk from*

Starting from the car park, go through the gate to Mottistone Down on Mottistone Estate, now owned by the National Trust, and straight ahead following a well-worn trail, passing several Bronze Age burial mounds.

The paths on the National Trust Land are not generally signposted or numbered but are well maintained and clear. If you get out of breath you can pretend you have stopped to admire the superb views, behind you, of the south-western side of the Island. To maintain the area and prevent gorse from taking over, the National Trust have begun grazing Highland cattle here. These gentle creatures make an interesting sight but dogs must be kept on a lead.

From the top you can see the Solent and get a good impression of how narrow the Solent becomes at Hurst Castle. On a clear day you should be able to see Swanage, and maybe even St Alban's Head, over to the

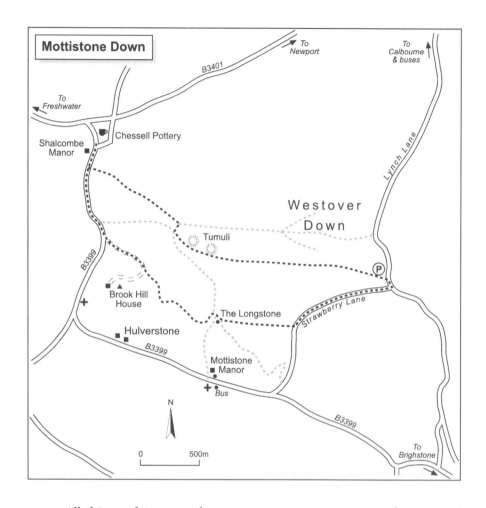

west. All this made it a good vantage point to use as part of a national beacon system in the Second World War. From the burial mounds, continue down hill to the next gate. You can often see kestrels hovering over the hillside here in search of prey. To your left you may catch a glimpse of the tall chimneys of Brook Hill House, once the home of JB Priestley.

Just before the gate, turn right along a bridle path into Brighstone Forest. After 50 yards take the first left and you will find yourself in a beech wood.

You may be able to hear a red squirrel scolding you as you pass through the trees. They come to the ground less often than their grey cousins and are rather smaller and more delicate in build. There are no grey squirrels on the Isle of Wight. A few years ago one did manage to swim across, the poor bedraggled thing was put on a ferry and taken straight back to the mainland. Beech grows well on the chalky soil here, this being part of the chalk ridge running from Swanage through the Isle of Wight across to Selsey Bill.

After about half a mile, at the end of this path, turn left, go through a gate and down the farm track to the road (B3399). Turn right, then walk about 250 yards along the road, past the charming old Shalcombe Manor, to Chessell Pottery. The café is in the courtyard of the pottery.

After your refreshment, return the way you came, back past Shalcombe Manor but continue along the road, past the path that brought you down, for about a quarter of a mile until you reach a driveway on your left flanked by hedges and well-mown grass.

This is the driveway to Brook Hill House, seen earlier from above, which has now been divided into several rather luxurious apartments.

You should see a sign, S39 to the Longstone, in the hedge. Go along this drive for about 200 yards to where the footpath (S39) leaves the drive, off to the left.

A little further along this path you will cross a stile which takes you onto Mottistone Common, open access land managed by the National Trust. The path then winds its way to the Longstone.

As part of the conservation programme New Forest ponies have been introduced here on a trial basis. So far they seem to be a success and are certainly popular with visitors. In the spring this is a lovely area to see bluebells, and at anytime of the year is a good place to see buzzards as they soar over the hills sloping away to your right. The 1987 hurricane caused much devastation here but also opened up some fantastic views as the close growing pines were knocked over like nine-pins.

As you move from chalk to sandstone you may notice a change in the vegetation. There is an array of acid–loving plants, including escaped

The Longstone

The Saxon 'Mottstone' or meeting stones, now known as the Longstone, are actually two large pieces of sandstone, one upright and the other lying at its feet, marking the site of a Neolithic longbarrow or burial chamber. The rest of the chamber has long since collapsed and been worn away. No one knows who brought them here, or why they should have chosen this place, but they are near the old highway, going over the top of the downs, and a Bronze Age track leads away from here down the hill. In the 1990s an Iron Age track was also discovered nearby, so it was obviously a meeting point of longstanding. It is also the site of pagan rituals and is said to be a focus for witchcraft around the times of the solstices. The Druids regard it as the most sacred site on the Island.

rhododendrons providing a lovely display in the spring, and purple heathers which are at their best in August. On your left you may recognise another burial mound on your way to the Longstone, although it is not as easy to distinguish as the ones seen earlier.

*As you pass this site, just in front of you and slightly to your right is a small rise known as Castle Hill and the remains of a Roman Castle and possibly an Iron Age Fort, although these are next to impossible to see because of the vegetation. However our path leads across the field in front of you. Follow this path for about a third of a mile until it reaches a small, but steep, road known as Strawberry Lane. Turn left and walk up the road for about half a mile, to its junction with Lynch Lane.

On your way you can see the remains of old quarry workings, including the arched entrance and the sloping track above, where the carts were pulled up to the yard. As you move back onto chalk you can see, in the warm, south-facing banks, sweet smelling wild marjoram, yellow common rock roses and purple scabious. You may also see some of the lovely chalkland butterflies such as the Chalkhill Blue and the Adonis Blue.

The Longstone

When you reach the end of Strawberry Lane the car park is just round the corner to your left.

Chessell Pottery Café
Tel: 01983 531248

These very popular tea rooms have plenty of tables both inside and outside in the courtyard, which is a very pleasant place to sit on a summer's day. The service is very friendly. They serve tea in generous sized pots of their own making and coffee in individual cafetieres or the usual array of espressos and cappuccinos. Their cake portions are also very generous, again served on their own china. The cakes and scones are always fresh and they also serve sandwiches and light lunches made with good quality, often local, ingredients, including Calbourne Classics clotted cream with the scones.

An added attraction is the pottery itself where you can even decorate a mug or plate and have it glazed as an unusual present to take back or, if you don't fancy lugging it around with you, have it posted.

Walk 15:
Freshwater Bay and Afton

Easy walking on downs and through a nature reserve, on footpaths and minor roads.

Distance	3 miles/5km
Start	Main car park in Freshwater Bay
Parking	Plenty of parking in Freshwater Bay, either in the pay and display car park or in adjacent Afton Road
Getting there by car	Freshwater bay is on the A 3055 at the eastern end of the Island
Getting there by bus	Bus number 12 from Freshwater and Newport stops in the bay about 200 yards north of the car park, next to the public toilets

Starting from the main car park in Freshwater Bay, head south up the hill, known as the Military Road, for about 200 yards.

Its name arose because it was originally built for the exclusive use of the Army to travel, between their numerous bases, all along this coast in World War II.

Turn left along Southdown Road, passing 'Totts Plot' on the left, a small piece of land donated to the National Trust to preserve the superb views. Then turn right into Freshwater Bay Golf Club along bridleway F32.

Keeping to the track go past several bungalows and the clubhouse, then through the gate. 100 yards past the clubhouse the path forks. Take the branch to the left, marked F32. 10 yards on, turn left and

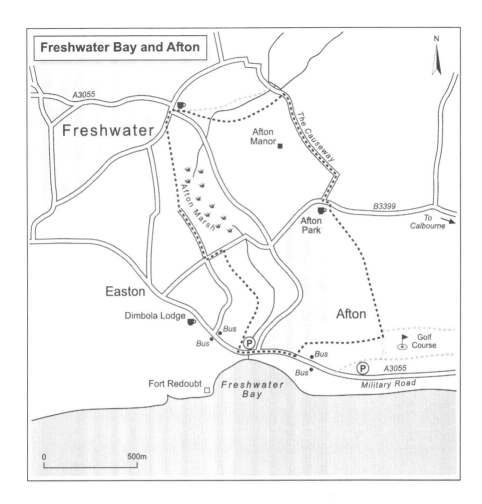

cross the grass to pass between two hedges into a field, following the sign for bridleway F31. Go straight ahead here, across the fields, passing paddocks to your right. The path eventually emerges onto a lane. Turn right to the main road B3399. The entrance to Afton Park is on the corner on your left, with the tea shop through the orchard, if you want to stop for tea at this point. If not, cross the road to the Causeway just to your left, which is also sign posted 'Freshwater Way'.

As you descend this narrow road, which was originally the only link with the western end of the Island, you will cross a stream flowing to your left and draining into Freshwater Bay. A few yards further on the Causeway Bridge crosses the Yar flowing to your right.

Thus, West Wight is nearly a separate island divided only by a short stretch of marsh.

When you reach the Causeway Bridge, take the first bridleway to the left, F61, which follows the old railway line.

As this is a marsh it may be muddy at times but it is fairly level and well gravelled. Whereas the Yar is tidal up to the Causeway, and hosts waders such as redshank, greenshank, oystercatchers, this part of the Yar is fresh and is home to a quite different set of wildlife. As well as the ubiquitous mallards you may see reed buntings, frogs and wild irises.

The path emerges next to the End of the Line Café, which is on the site of the old railway terminus.

Freshwater Bay

On leaving the café turn right, cross the road and then turn left up Stroud Road. After about 100 yards, the footpath, F37, goes off to the left (opposite the recreation ground). It feels a little disconcerting to be walking through someone's garden, but it is the right path. Cross a field and then over a stile into another garden. The path goes straight ahead through a gate on the other side, then follow the path for 200 yards.

When you reach a lane turn left, following the Freshwater Way sign, then left again at the junction, still following the Freshwater Way signs.

A little further down the road, just before you cross the bridge, Black Bridge, there are two turnings off to the right. The first is marked F36, the second, 30 yards further on, marked only with a wooden sign, is a slightly prettier route through Afton Marsh Nature Reserve, which is an SSSI; the two paths join after a short distance.

Keep to the path to avoid damaging any plants. The path is well maintained with boardwalks through the wettest parts. It wends its way through the Nature Reserve for about half a mile emerging in Coastguard Lane, which leads you out once more to Freshwater Bay.

The bay is a favourite spot in rough weather when the sea crashes onto the rocks and, at high tide, onto the sea wall by the Albion Hotel (whose bar WH Auden and Christopher Isherwood once frequented), sending spray shooting into the air. If the sun is in the right place you can see rainbows in the spray.

On the right, and overloooking the bay, is Fort Redoubt, a reminder of how seriously the British Government took the threat from Napoleon, one of many fortifications built on the South Coast. Lower down you can see an entrance in the cliff reached by an iron ladder, an access to the fort from the sea. It was in regular use until the middle of the last century.

Freshwater Bay is also home to the Freshwater Lifeboat, which is supported entirely by local contributions as it is not funded by the RNLI. When the bay is busy the station is often open so you can see how the boat is launched and recovered.

Afton Park
Summer open every day 10am-4pm
Winter open Wednesday to Sunday 10am–4pm
Thursday to Saturday also open 5.30-9.30 pm
Tel: 01983 755774

The entrance to the **Apple Tree Café** is through the orchard and beautiful gardens, set in a designated Area Of Outstanding Natural Beauty. There are tables inside, outside in the courtyard or in the gardens. They serve an interesting range of cakes often featuring apples, unsurprisingly, but also offering gluten-free options. They also serve light lunches and snacks using their own produce as much as possible. The service is friendly and helpful and the café provides a delightful place to relax in a superb setting.

The End of the Line Café
Open all year 10am-4pm

This is a very popular place with visitors and locals alike, being quite economical and serving good homemade food, including cakes and light lunches. (It is also right next to the local supermarket and the garden centre). The café is filled with station memorabilia and photos and has a nice homey atmosphere, with seating inside and out. In spring you can be serenaded by the birds in the marsh next to the terrace. It is the sort of place you can arrive at with muddy boots, dogs, children and it will be okay. Portions are a generous size and service is prompt and efficient.

Walk 16:
Tennyson Down and the Needles

Coastal walk. Mostly good paths on chalk downs but can be slippery in wet weather.

Distance	6½ miles/10.5km
Start	The bus stop, next to the public toilets
Parking	There is a large pay and display car park in Freshwater Bay, or park in Afton Road next to the car park
Getting there by car	Freshwater bay is on the A 3055 at the eastern end of the Island
Getting there by bus	Bus number 12 from Freshwater and Newport, the bus stop is about 200 yards north of the car park, next to the public toilets

The walk starts by the bus stop, next to the public toilets which are clearly signposted. After 50 yards, a footpath leads off this track to the right and is clearly marked Coastal Path.

As you cross the field, to the left is Fort Redoubt, part of the Island's former defences. In the summer this is a wonderful place to hear skylarks.

The path leads out onto Tennyson Down, a smooth walk over the short turf which grows on the chalk. The views here, back across the Island are superb and, on a clear day, you should easily be able to see as far as St Catherine's Down in the south.

The cliffs provide nesting places for hundreds of birds, including kittiwakes and the rare, but exciting, peregrine falcons. Although a

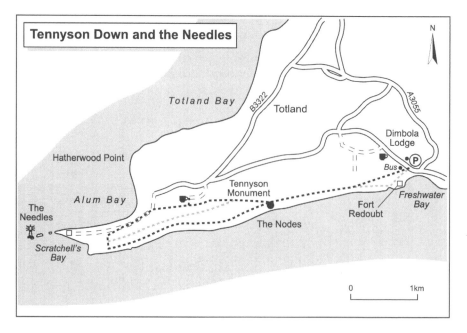

pigeon can out-fly a peregrine in a straight race, these falcons can dive
at speeds of up to 270mph to catch their prey, often coming out of the
sun, giving the pigeon no chance! In the summer you may well see the
strikingly marked wheatears standing on top of little mounds and
clumps, checking you out. You may also see yellow hammers, especially
near the gorse bushes, with their distinctive call of 'a little-bit-of-bread-
and-no-cheese'. Look out also for chalkland butterflies such as the
Chalkhill Blue, Adonis Blue and Marbled White. Plant life here includes
yellow wort, early gentians and the pretty harebells.

As you reach the Tennyson Monument, the views widen out to include
the western half of the Island with the chalk ridge that forms the
'backbone' clearly visible. Nearer at hand is the Yar estuary, winding
its way towards Freshwater Bay in its attempt to cut off this end of the
Isle of Wight. Further away to the north you can see the New Forest,
and may be able to see the South Downs beyond. There is a good view
from here of Hurst Spit, jutting out towards the Island with its castle
and lighthouse on the promontory, like a gate to the Solent. To the west
are the cliffs of Purbeck, which are part of the same Cretaceous chalk
ridge as Tennyson Down.

The monument itself is made of a piece of Iona Granite. It was put here in 1897 in memory of Alfred, Lord Tennyson who lived just off the downs, to your right, and loved to walk up here. Set on the highest part of the down, the monument is visible from quite a distance and replaced an earlier seamark, the remnants of which are by the beacon a little further on.

From the monument take the path to the left, leading on to the West High Down.

Chalk cliffs are quite crumbly and liable to sudden falls (otherwise the Needles wouldn't exist) so you do need to exercise some caution.

On this part of the walk you will see earthworks and strange flattened areas. These are gun emplacements and the remains of military buildings from the Second World War. The whole of this coast was heavily defended to protect the entrance to the Solent and both Southampton and Portsmouth docks and, although all the brickwork has been removed from this area, it has been hard to eradicate all traces.

Fort Redoubt

Fort Redoubt was built in 1855 at a time when there were still fears of a French invasion. It is not open to the public but the main layout can still be observed from above, on the Downs. A deep, brick lined ditch was cut to the north and west in order to stop an attack from the land. The cliffs themselves providing adequate defence seaward. Inside the ditch was a barrack block, designed to house 24 soldiers. On the top of the newly created 'island' was a parade ground and a one-storey flat roofed building, providing officers quarters. Extensive tunnels and rooms were built into the chalk cliff in order to be safe from mortars. Various guns were kept at the fort over the years, but in the 1914-1918 war only the lower battery was armed.

The fort was restricted in size and so, in 1928, was sold to Mrs Amelia Bowland Cross for £600. Since then it has had several owners and at one time was run as tea rooms, but sadly has since reverted to a private residence.

The Needles in windy weather with the sea breaking into Scratchells Bay

After one-and-a-half miles, as you reach the end of the Downs, climb over the stile and head on past the aerial.

Below is further evidence of the Island's military past and there is lots to see here. On the upper part is the New Battery (entrance free) and there is also an exhibition about the Black Knight and Black Arrow space rocket engines, built on the Island and tested here, prior to the rockets being shipped to Woomera in Australia for launching. The rocket test site itself is on the cliff edge and next to it is a viewpoint for the famous Needles and their lighthouse. The lighthouse was one of the last to be manned, hence the helipad on the top, which was an easier way to get out there in bad weather than taking a small boat close to the treacherous rocks. Next to the test site is a coastguard station which, although maintained, is no longer regularly manned; technology has replaced the human eye.

On the very end is the Needles Old Battery, completed in1863, and now owned by the National Trust, another example of anti-French fortifications, which show how seriously the government of the day took the threat of an invasion. If you are a member, it is worth a visit and they do have a tiny café in the Old Look-out Tower, which, although not much to write home about in terms of refreshments, does have a spectacular view.

When you are ready to return, take the road or the footpath below the coastguard cottages, back towards Alum Bay.

The walk provides an excellent view of the famous multi-coloured sandstone cliffs. In the past, enthusiastic holiday makers wanting a memento collected their own samples, but people inevitably scraped it from the lower parts, causing the cliffs above to collapse. Nowadays, only authorised collectors are allowed to remove sand from the cliff, but the shop on the cliff top does allow you to fill your own lighthouse or paperweight with sand they have collected. At the other end of the Island exactly identical geological features appear in the cliffs, but for some reason they have escaped the ravages inflicted here, not the least of which is the 'Pleasure Park'. This used to be a rather lovely area, with only a small monument marking the place where Marconi first transmitted radio signals to a ship in the bay below. The monument is still there, but it is pretty hard to find amidst the merry-go-rounds.

However, it isn't actually necessary to traipse through this misplaced fairground because, while the road turns sharply left as it approaches Alum Bay, there is a footpath on this bend, which is signposted T25; there is also a sign for the tea rooms. Follow this path along the hedge and you will shortly see another sign for Warren Farm Tea Rooms. A few yards further on is a path leading down to the left to the farmhouse for your refreshment. It is clearly marked with one of the teashop's own signs.

When you have finished your tea, return to the path and continue along the lower slopes of the West High Down for about a third of a mile to a stile.

Just over the stile is a half-size replica of the first seamark, together with the remains of the original, that used to stand in the vicinity of the Tennyson Monument, which were moved here when the new monument was erected. The top part was designed to be used as a

Julia Margaret Cameron and Dimbola Lodge

The poet Henry Taylor wrote of Dimbola Lodge "...a house indeed to which everyone resorted for pleasure, and in which no man, woman or child was ever known to be unwelcome".

Julia Margaret Cameron, a pioneering photographer, welcomed to Dimbola the cream of Victorian society, including Ellen Terry, Charles Darwin, Lewis Carroll, Edward Lear, Holman Hunt and, of course, Tennyson. Cameron was born in India, educated in Europe then returned to India where she met and married her husband Charles. They stayed there until his retirement when they moved to London. Here she became part of the Kensington artistic set and met Lord Tennyson who invited her to Farringford. She loved it and within a few weeks had bought two cottages next to Tennyson's estate, which she converted into a single residence by adding a gothic tower between them. She named the house Dimbola Lodge after the family's tea plantation in India.

Three years later, when she was 48, her daughter gave her a camera as a present. The gift sparked a passion that became almost an obsession. As well as her family, she photographed all her visitors and friends, some, such as Tennyson, many times.

Although at the time Cameron was seen as an unconventional and experimental photographer, her images have a solid place in the history of photography. Many were deliberately out of focus as she strove to capture her ideas of beauty. She wrote, "I longed to arrest all the beauty that came before me and at length the longing has been satisfied". Her work had a huge impact on the development of modern photography, especially her closely cropped portraits, which are still mimicked today. And at a time when photography was in its infancy, hers are the only photographs we have of many historical figures of the age.

As well as the tea rooms, Dimbola now houses a second-hand bookshop, a gift shop and a well respected photographic museum, which stages exhibitions by both local and international photgraphers. There is a charge for entrance to the museum.

beacon in bad weather. It was brought back into use when it formed part of a chain of beacons across the country, lit to mark the Queen's Silver Jubilee.

From the stile take the path to the right, back up to the Tennyson Monument and then retrace your steps to Freshwater Bay.

As you return across the last field to the main road, you may notice an odd building with a tower in the middle of it. This is Dimbola Lodge, once the home of Julia Margaret Cameron, a pioneering photographer and friend of Lord Tennyson. The house is now a museum and gallery, which often stages interesting exhibitions by well known photographers. It also has an excellent restaurant and tea rooms.

Warren Farm Tea Rooms
Open April to October, Saturday to Thursday, 12.00-5.30 pm
Tel: 01983 753200

You can't really miss the place because, apart from the fact that it is the only farm for several miles, there are usually hordes of people making the same pilgrimage – it is deservedly popular and I always feel I have had a proper day out after I've been here.

Warren Farm tea rooms is a family-run business, on a working farm, serving delicious homemade cakes and scones baked in an Aga, generous sized pots of tea and cream teas with proper clotted cream. *The Guardian* ranked their teas as one of the top ten cream teas in the country (what a job to have).

You can sit inside, outside in the courtyard or up in the gardens looking across the fields. There is even a toy farm and animals for the children to play with. Rather unusually, you order your teas at the kitchen window. I like the way they have adapted the building to the needs of the business, whilst retaining the farmhouse feel. Service is prompt and friendly and the staff are very accommodating if you have particular needs or can't manage your tray.

A fascinating innovation is the little shop in the farmyard which, as well as selling the usual cakes and biscuits, local arts and crafts and souvenirs, has begun selling takeaway cream teas; these are boxes containing frozen scones, jam and cream which take about an hour to defrost, perfect to take to the beach.

Cameron Tea Rooms, Dimbola Lodge

Open 10am-5pm daily in school holidays. 10am-4pm Tuesday to Sunday in the winter (last orders half an hour before closing)
Tel: 01983 756814

Dimbola, named after Julia Margaret Cameron's plantation in India, has a restaurant and tea rooms on the ground floor, in a very pleasant room with views back towards the bay; there are also tables outside. There are usually interesting photography displays around the walls to entertain you while you wait for your food. They serve superb, and often out of the ordinary, cakes and also do very tasty lunch dishes, vegetarian options being a particular speciality, using local produce where possible.

The tea rooms have the unhurried feel of another age, as though you were in Cameron's lounge taking tea. Service is polite and helpful and the food nicely presented. Although not cheap, it is worth the money.

Walk 17:
Colwell and Freshwater

Downs walk with military history on footpaths and by-ways.

Distance	7 miles/11km
Start	Colwell Bay at the end of Colwell Chine Road
Parking	There is plenty of parking in Colwell Chine Road and in the car park at the end of the road
Getting there by car	Colwell is on the A3054 between Yarmouth and Totland; the turning to the bay is almost opposite The Colwell Bay Inn
Getting there by bus	Bus number 7 from Yarmouth stops opposite Colwell Chine Road, leading to the bay

Begin in Colwell Bay at the end of Colwell Chine Road. There are two paths to Totland, but the nicest is to go down to the sea front and turn left along the esplanade. This takes you to the first of four cafés on this walk, Crusoe's.

The esplanade continues round the corner into Totland Bay, passing the remains of WWII defences.

As you round this corner you get your first sight of the famous Needles and their lighthouse. Both Colwell and Totland beaches are very popular as they are sandy and sheltered, particularly from the strong tides that rip through the narrow entrance to the Solent. Totland Bay has its own pier, built in the Victorian era when pier-building was all the rage. Trips ran from here around the Solent and to the mainland,

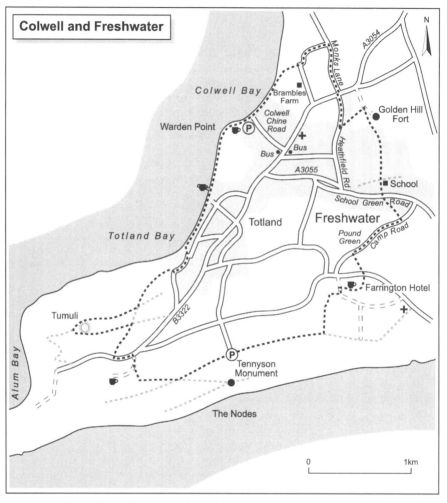

Colwell and Freshwater

on and off, until 1969. Since then it has had a succession of owners but, like so many piers around the country, the high cost of maintenance has led to the pier's inevitable decay. The current owners hope to be able to restore it but so far have only been able to do the part nearest the cafe, which they use as an outdoor seating area. This is the second café on the walk. It is a typical beachside affair with teas and ice-creams, etc. to take away or eat there. In the summer it is open seven days a week until 8.30, but has more limited opening times at other times of the year, largely dictated by the weather.

Continue along the Esplanade.

At the far end is the old Totland lifeboat house which was in use from 1885 to 1924. On the wall is a poem explaining when tides will be high in this bay, which is quite useful.

Poem on the side of the boathouse

Walk up the steps next to it and, at the top, turn right. After about 200 yards, turn right onto the footpath sign posted to Alum Bay (no number). This takes you through some shady woodland out onto Headon (pronounced *hee'dn*) Warren.

The Warren is different to most other downs areas on the Island, as it is sandstone and, therefore, more acidic than the chalky downs elsewhere. In summer the heather is fantastic and you can often see kestrels using the lift off the hillside. The Warren gets its name from its use as a rabbit breeding area in the 15th century.

There are lots of paths through the Warren but, for the visitor, the best way is to go to the top where there are spectacular views of the Solent. To get there, when you emerge from the trees, walk pretty much straight on until you reach an information board. Take the path just to the left of the board, heading ever upwards.

From the top you can get a good idea of the narrowness of the entrance to the Solent, with the long Hurst Spit ending in its 16th century castle and white lighthouse, erected about the same time as the Needles light, and, on the Island shore, Fort Warden, a Victorian construction. The tides through this gap can be as much as 4 ½ knots (1 knot = 1 nautical mile per hour) as the depth drops sharply to around 10 fathoms (60 metres). You should be able to tell the direction of the tides by the number of boats going in that direction, but it is fun to watch a yacht struggling up against the tide.

On the summit are Bronze Age burial mounds and from here there is a good view of the Needles.

The Needles

The Needles are a set of jagged lumps of chalk jutting out of the westernmost point of the Island, very similar to the Old Harry rocks running out to the east of Swanage, of which they are a continuation. Their name derives from a tall thin, needle like rock which stood in the middle of the line. This pillar collapsed in a storm in 1764, with a crash so loud it was heard on the mainland, leaving a gap, but the name has stuck. At high tide and in a shallow draft boat, it is possible to 'thread the needle', i.e. sail between the rocks, but there are more than a few who have come to grief trying. A few years ago one pair of intrepid rock climbers actually swam and climbed right out to the lighthouse.

The first Needles light tower was built on the cliff top in 1786 but, as the light was 470 feet above sea level, it was often obscured by sea mists and fogs and was therefore of limited use to mariners. In 1859, a new one was built on the outermost rock with the lower walls over a metre thick. Much of the base rock was cut away to form the foundation, and cellars and storehouses were excavated in the chalk. Until 1994, the lighthouse was powered by 100V DC electricity from its own generators. The keepers left for the last time, in December of that year, when it was automated, and now an undersea cable provides mains power.

Go round the burial mound, passing another information board, and take the path on the south side, then take the path down to the right, heading east again. This takes you past an underground reservoir. After 200 yards, the path forks by a wooden sign post, turn right here and continue down hill to a stile and across a field to the Alum Bay New Road, going to the right of the house. Turn left here. Crossing the road at the junction, you will see Alum Bay Old Road, a road to Warren House Farm (tea shop described in walk 14) and between them an unmade track. Take this latter, or the footpath that runs parallel to it. Go over the stile at the end and turn left. The path here climbs slightly to an old fashioned beacon, replicating the one that once stood on top of the downs. Once over the stile next to it take the track to the left, downhill.

You are now on the lower parts of Tennyson Down, part of the chalk ridge that once stretched across to Swanage. This is characterised by hawthorn, elder and especially beech, which thrives on the chalky soil. In early summer look out for patches of the beautiful early gentian.

When you reach the quarry, where there is a small car park, carry straight on across the little access road. Further on you will see a track to your left, ignore this and carry on until the path forks, marked by blue and yellow arrows. Take the left-hand fork, go over the stile and after a few yards another stile, and along a path between some fences, at the end of which turn right by a footpath sign. This brings you out onto Green Lane and the wall of the Farringford Estate. Turn left here. After about 100 yards, just after the cattle grid, turn right onto a track into the grounds of the Farringford , the fourth of the tea rooms.

After your tea, leave The Farringford along the main drive. Take footpath F41, almost opposite the entrance, just to the left of

Colwell Bay

Farringford Lodge, to Pound Green. When you reach the little green turn right along Camp Road. After about half a mile, just after Jubilee Close, turn left along footpath F21 to Station Road taking you across the recreation ground. On reaching the main road, cross over, and just to your left is a sign to bridleway F18 to Golden Hill. This goes up the side of a school, behind which you need to turn right, then immediately left up a hill. This climbs all the way up to Golden Hill Fort, which is a large hexagonal structure currently undergoing extensive renovations.

The fort was built in 1886, as a barracks for soldiers serving on the local batteries of Fort Victoria and the Needles. In 1986, it was sold to the council and turned into industrial units. When the industrial units shut down, the Fort fell into a period of abandonment and the Grade I listed monument was put onto the English Heritage critical list. It is now being converted into luxury apartments.

When you reach the fort entrance, turn sharp left and head down hill through the copse for about a third of a mile. At the bottom of the hill, where the path levels out, turn right onto footpath F14. which takes you to a road (Heathfield Road). Turn right here for 200 yards to the junction with the A 3054. Cross straight over and go along Monks Lane for about 600 yards, to the holiday village, then turn left and follow the Coastal Path until you reach footpath F13, which you follow to the sea. Finish with a stroll back along the beach, don't be put off, there are steps over the highest groynes!

Crusoe's, Colwell Bay
Tel: 01983 759333

Crusoe's boasts that it is open 365 days a year. It is as much a way of life for the owners, who are a local family, as a business. It is a cheap and cheerful beach café with the usual snacks and ice-creams, lots of tea and homemade cakes. It is certainly not posh but it is very friendly and the staff considerate. They even have a little dog house outside for your pet to shelter in. Portions are generous and they have tables inside and out or you can opt for take away and sit on the sea wall. It is a popular place for locals as well as tourists.

Farringford, Freshwater
Open all year
Tel: 01983 752500

The Farringford is best known as Tennyson's home. It is set in a large estate and tea is served either on the terrace or in the lounge overlooking his garden and with views of Brook Down and Freshwater Bay or in a specially built summer house in the gardens. Tea is waiter served in china teapots and coffee comes in a cafetiere. The cream teas are highly recommended.

The Farringford has recently been extensively restored in honour of the poet's centenary; many original features have been preserved, including the beautiful panelling and fireplaces. As you sit here it is easy to imagine him strolling out onto the downs named after him, or drinking tea with his guests,

Entrance to Farringford,
Tennyson's home

who included many of the great thinkers and writers of the day; people such as Charles Darwin, Garibaldi, Charles Dodgson (Lewis Carroll), artist William Holman Hunt, John Ruskin, Henry Longfellow, Edward Lear, Sir Arthur Sullivan, actress Ellen Terry and, of course, Julia Margaret Cameron along with an assortment of politicians, professors and duchesses. Cameron lived in Dimbola Lodge next door to Farringford and was a pioneering photographer of the 19th Century. In her studio she photographed many of Tennyson's friends and guests. These give an invaluable insight into the life of Alfred Lord Tennyson and the importance of Farringford as a source of inspiration to many of the most influential people of the 19th Century.

Walk 18:
Fort Victoria, Yarmouth

Coastal walk mostly on level footpaths, short section on roads.

Distance	3 miles/5km
Start	Car park at Fort Victoria Country Park
Parking	Large free car park at Fort Victoria Country Park
Getting there by car	Fort Victoria is just off the A3054 to the west of Yarmouth
Getting there by bus	Bus number 7 from Yarmouth stops at the top of the road leading to the fort, West Hill Lane, and start the walk from *

Starting from the car park go to the shore and head east along the beach, passing a derelict pier. This leads you along to the sea wall past Norton Grange Coastal Resort, to Norton Spit.

Norton Spit is a Site of Special Scientific Interest (SSSI) which protects and, in fact, creates Yarmouth Harbour. It provides a wonderful wildlife haven for salt-tolerant plants such as sea lavender and sea holly. It also provides a feeding ground for birds such as greenshank, shelduck and several types of geese.

Unless you want to take a stroll around the spit, turn right here up to the main road. On the road turn left and, where the pavement finishes, cross over and go up Gas Works Lane, also designated footpath F1, for about 300 yards. After the second house, take footpath F2 to the right. At the top of the slope go over the stile and down a narrow path to meet the road again. Turn left here, then after 200 yards turn right down West hill Lane towards Fort Victoria Country Park again.

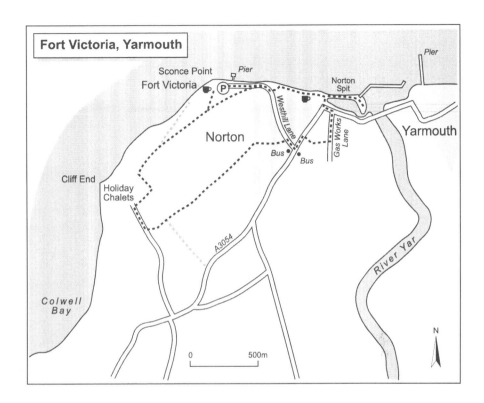

* About 100 yards down the lane take the second turning on the left, Linstone Drive, which is marked as a footpath, F3 Monks Lane. After about 200 yards the footpath goes off to the left between house numbers 13 and 15. There is a signpost, but it is often overhung with branches. The path through the fields however is well-worn and clear.

The uncultivated grassland makes it a popular place for kestrels and there are usually several to be seen, as well as green woodpeckers. Listen too for the 'zee' of the greenfinches and the 'little-bit-of-bread-and-no-cheese' of the yellowhammers.

At the end of this path. turn right on to a small road, following the Coastal Path signs. After 200 yards, take the next right, at the entrance to the holiday camp, marked 'Coastal Path'. This path leads you back down to Fort Victoria Country Park. There are various routes through the woodland; for easy walking stick to the main path, otherwise there

Fort Victoria

Although one might expect a fort to be high, for visibility and firing down onto the enemy, the narrowness of the channel meant that Fort Victoria could be designed to house a large number of guns which could be fired from low down, piercing the sides of enemy ships and sinking them quickly. It was a clever idea, although it never had to be put into practice.

The area had suffered frequent attacks by the French until Henry VIII built Hurst Castle, opposite and Yarmouth Castle on the Island, as part of major south coast fortifications. Hurst Castle was modernised during the Napoleonic wars, at which point it was decided that further fortifications were needed on the island shore to complement Hurst. Forts Albert and Victoria were completed in the 1850s, and remained in use as barracks until the last soldiers left in 1962, although they never fired a shot in anger.

The fort now houses a very good underwater archaeological museum, an aquarium, a planetarium and a model railway exhibition, as well as toilets and a café.

are pleasant paths that wind their way between the trees, although some care needs to be taken as coastal erosion has removed some routes. On the main path, the sign pointing to refreshments and toilets will lead you back to Fort Victoria.

Café Verdi, Fort Victoria

Open every day from Easter to October, 9am-5pm
Tel: 01983 761777

In the summer the café is a bustling, cheery place, serving simple but good quality food, much of it made using local produce. The portions are generous and the service friendly and efficient. There is a good variety of tasty cakes to choose from. Cold and hot lunches are also available. Tea is served in metal tea pots or in mugs or cups. Fresh filter coffee is available or the usual options of espressos and cappuccinos, etc.

The café is housed in the fort itself and has windows looking out to the Solent, so you can imagine what it must have been like for the soldiers housed here, or you can sit outside looking towards Hurst Castle less than a mile away across the water. The sudden narrowing of the channel causes the tide to flow very quickly, so it is not safe to swim here. The fast tides have scoured out a deep channel making it a great place to be if there is a yacht race – they come surprisingly close.

The Boathouse
Open April to October, Tuesday to Sunday 9.30am-3.30pm

100 yards back up the road from Fort Victoria is The Boathouse, which is a little bit more sophisticated than Café Verdi, although they have more limited opening hours. They serve breakfasts and luncheons as well as afternoon tea with a small array of cakes. The tea is fine, although you don't get hot water with it. You can sit inside in the

Looking across to Hurst Castle

modernised boathouse itself, in the gardens or on decking on the beach, with the waves crashing beside you only a few feet away.

Norton Grange
Open all year
Tel: 01983 760323

Right next to Norton Spit Site of Special Scientific Interest (SSSI), the hotel is part of the Warners group and has the sort of fare one would expect in a large hotel. It lacks some of the personal touch, but the tea is fine and they serve Costa coffee. The limited array of cakes are pleasant and a reasonable portion size. What is lovely, is being able to sit outside on the newly built decking overlooking the Solent and the harbour entrance. There is often yacht racing going on at the weekends, which adds to the entertainment.

Walk 19:
Yarmouth and the Causeway

Level walking, good for wildlife watching. First half has good, flat paths suitable for wheelchairs; second half has footpaths and bridleways.

Distance	4½ miles/7.25km
Start	Yarmouth Car Park
Parking	There is a large pay and display car park in the town
Getting there by car	Yarmouth is on the A3054, 9 miles west of Newport
Getting there by bus	Bus number 7 from Newport

Starting from Yarmouth Car Park, take the path south along by the side of the river. Just before the path meets the cycle way is the old tide mill, a large four storey building, now a private home.

This part of the estuary is an excellent place for bird watching at low tide. The mud flats provide food for hundreds of waders, including oyster-catchers, greenshank, and egrets, which have in recent years begun to breed here.

Just to the left, behind the tide mill, is the former station, but our route takes us right, along the cycleway.

This follows the route of the old railway line which joined West Wight with Newport, from 1889 to 1966, but was closed in the, now infamous, Beeching cuts.

Continue along the path until you reach the Causeway. This first part is suitable for pushchairs and wheel chairs.

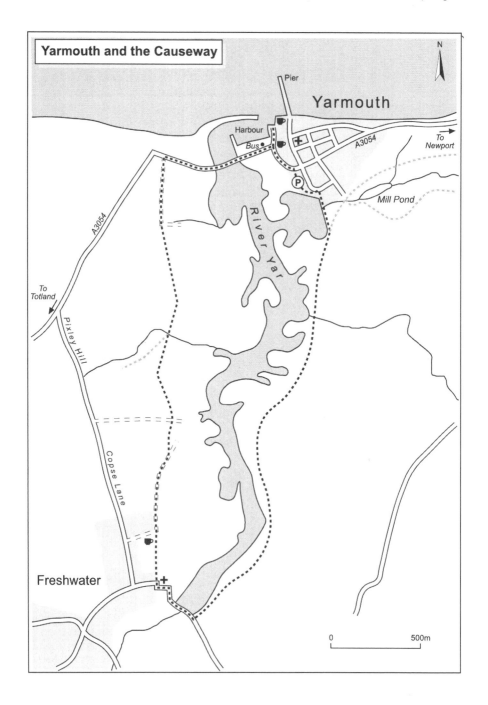

Yarmouth and the Causeway

N

Pier

Yarmouth

Harbour

Bus

A3054

To
Newport

P

Mill Pond

River Yar

A3054

To
Totland

Pixley Hill

Copse Lane

Freshwater

0   500m

Yarmouth harbour

Until the bridge over the Yar, in Yarmouth, was built, the Causeway was the main route to the west of the Isle of Wight. Hence the pill-box to your right, built in World War II when there was a large Army base here. The western end of the island was thus closed to non-resident civilians. You had to have a pass even to visit family members.

Turn right, walk over the Causeway Bridge, past the pill-box and continue up Hooke Hill, named after the scientist Robert Hooke, to All Saints Church, where his father was vicar. Follow the finger post F1 (Freshwater Way) on your right, which crosses in front of the church.

The graveyard, which contains mounds dating back to 1693, is a wonderful wildlife haven, with plenty of mature trees, and has been managed in such a way as to encourage wild flowers.

The path continues on past here to Kings Manor Farm Shop and Café.

After the farm shop, the path joins a tarmaced section and is clearly signposted F1. 500 yards along here you reach Kings Manor Farm itself. At the entrance the path turns left over a double stile and bridge. The path through the field is well worn and is signposted clearly. Go over another stile and, after 100 yards, through a kissing gate. Turn left and go up the track without a cattle grid for about 200

The Causeway Bridge

yards until the path dips down to a small copse. As you reach the trees, look for footpath F1 off to the right.

Walk through the copse, over a stile into the next field, keeping to the left-hand side of the field, over another stile, in the corner, and across the next field, keeping just to the left of the fence. The path is well worn and carefully left clear of crops and takes you to a stile into Saltern Wood. After about 200 yards the path emerges onto an unmade road, called Gas Works Lane.

A surprisingly industrial name for such a rural place, the gasworks have long since gone but even now, unbeknown to the casual observer, there is a thriving boatyard at the end of this lane.

Turn left onto the lane and this will lead you to the main road.

When you reach the road turn right over the swing bridge. As you cross the bridge look out for a short, but substantial, wooden pier on your left, which is all that is left of the old bridge.

Yarmouth has a lifeboat and you will probably see it on your left in the harbour, if it is not out on a call. Yarmouth lifeboat station operates the largest class of lifeboat, the Severn class, and covers the western end of the Solent. The Solent is a very busy stretch of water and it is not uncommon to hear and see the maroon go up, calling the lifeboat men, although nowadays they are also contacted by more modern methods like mobile phones and pagers!

Most of the tea rooms are in the centre of the town, in or around St James' Square, near the church, which is visible from the car park.

King Manor Farm Shop

Copse Lane, Freshwater, PO40 9TL
Open Monday to Saturday 9am-5pm, Sunday 9am-4pm.
Tel: 01983 754401

This is a fairly new venture for the owners of Kings Manor Farm and, at the time of writing, still needed a bit of refining, but they haven't taken the easy option of buying in cakes and snacks and have instead come up with some interesting and unusual ideas. They also serve light lunches and salads, including burgers made with their own Aberdeen Angus beef. Tables outside offer lovely views of the Yar valley and the downs, inside the room is half café and half shop. The place is very clean and the staff are enthusiastic and helpful.

Jireh Tea rooms, St James' Square

Open all year. Serving from morning coffee to evening meals
Tel: 01983 760513

This house dates back to the 17th Century and was once a part of the Town Hall, next door. It has a charming, traditional feel, with lovely home-made cakes and waiter service. You have a choice of seating, at a conventional table, in the conservatory or on leather sofas in front of the fireplace.

Jireh House, 17th Century Guest House and Tearooms

Coming here always feels like a real treat, something not to be rushed. They also run a guest house here.

Gossips, St James' Square
Open all year 8.45am -6.00pm in summer
They may shut earlier at other times
Tel: 01983 760646

A slightly cheaper alternative to the Jireh tea rooms, Gossips is at the end of the square, next to the pier, where you can watch the comings and goings on the Solent. Having a good view of the harbour entrance makes this a favourite place to await the ferry to Lymington, especially if it is cold and wet. This is a more basic, café style establishment but they serve a good variety of reasonably priced scones and cakes, and also operate a very popular ice-cream kiosk. They have plenty of seating inside and out, and they do takeaway so you can sit on the little beach next to the café instead. It has a relaxed, friendly feel and is popular with locals as well as tourists.

The Mariner Coffee House, St James' Square
Open all year 9am-5pm
Tel: 01983 761021

Another option, on the other side of the Old Town hall to the Jireh Tea rooms, is The Mariner which, as its name might suggest, has a nautical theme. You can sit in the windows and watch the bustle of the square over your cuppa. It is waitress served and they boast fresh, home made cakes, of which they have a good array and can serve breakfast, lunch and tea. However the tea comes in rather small pots (only one and a half cups), and there are no outside tables.

Choclat'ere, Wheatsheaf Lane, Yarmouth
Open all year 9am-5pm
Tel: 01983 761640

This is a chocolaterie that also serves really good quality coffee and tea and rather lovely hot chocolate. They have a small array of fresh cakes, generally loaf cakes, and cookies. They also serve Calbourne Classics ice cream. Serve is friendly and charming. They have a couple of tables inside and three or four outside.

Walk 20:
Newtown and Shalfleet

Good wildlife walk. Level walking on bridlepaths, footpaths and road, some stiles.

Distance	7½ miles/12km
Start	The National Trust car park in Newtown
Parking	The National Trust car park in Newtown, opposite the old Town Hall
Getting there by car	Newtown is on the coast half way between Cowes and Yarmouth. Turn off the A3054 just to the west of Shalfleet and look for the brown signs to Newtown Town Hall
Getting there by bus	Number 12 bus stops in Shalfleet, start from * near the end of the walk

From the car park turn left, then take footpath CB13a on the right, next to 'Francheville'.

'Francheville' was the village pub for 200 years, until 1916, and is the oldest surviving building in Newtown. The sign on the house is Newtown's thirteenth century Common Seal.

This footpath runs fairly straight, and parallel to the road, 'Gold Street', for about half a mile, following approximately the line of the former High Street, across the fields to emerge, through a kissing gate, opposite Walter's Copse on Town Gate Lane. Turn right here and walk along the lane.

Near Old Vicarage Lane was the Town Gate, one of the two medieval gateways to Newtown. Now it is hard to believe the town was so large. White Admiral butterflies are common in this area.

At the end of this lane turn left onto the road. Walk along here for about half a mile then turn right into Coleman's Lane. After 150 yards, turn right onto a track used as a bridleway, marked CB26, to Swainston. After 300 yards, bear right to cross a small bridge then at the next junction, follow the bridleway sign to Three Gates Farm and the Lazy Cow Café.

By the farm shop turn left and continue through the farm to the main road, the A3054. Cross the road and follow the track to Swainston Manor, bridleway CB27. After about half a mile the track forks. Take the right-hand branch over a small bridge, to cross the now dismantled railway line to Freshwater. Continue straight, and slightly uphill, for another quarter of a mile, until you reach a footpath on your right at the end of the woods, which is not numbered but does have a sign.

The path passes round the Swainston Manor estate. In earlier years the whole walk would be through the manorial lands, which extended to

Newtown Harbour

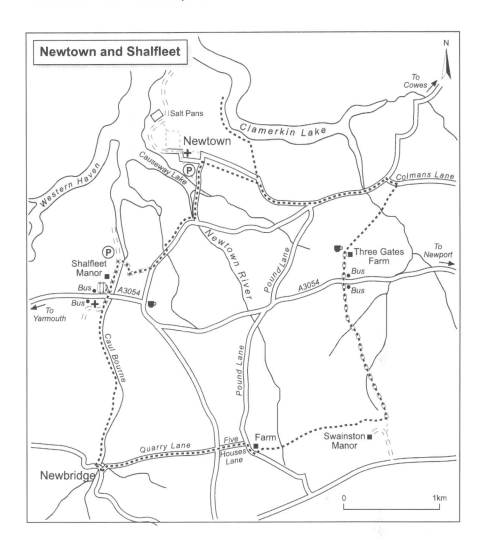

Newtown in the north and about the same distance again to the south of the manor.

After leaving the woodland, the path crosses some farmland and continues in a fairly straight line for a little under a mile, along the edge of one field then across the middle of the next, where the farmer has helpfully cleared a path through the crops.

Newtown

It is hard to believe now, that this tiny village was once a bustling sea port, the capital of the Isle of Wight and returned two MPs to parliament.

The faint traces of ridge and furrow cultivation in the area suggest that it has been a human settlement for a long time. The whole area was part of the ecclesiastical manor of Calbourne which, in AD827, was given to the Bishops of Winchester by King Egbert. Successive bishops invested heavily in the area and built a summer palace at Swainston. By this time its prosperity was already attracting invaders, one of whom was Sweyn (father of Canute) who sacked Newtown in 1001 and after whom Swainston is named. No lasting damge was done, however, as the Domesday Survey listed Swainston Manor, which included Newtown, as the largest and richest on the Island.

In 1285, Edward I visited Swainston Manor and picked a quarrel with the Bishop of Winchester, almost certainly with the intention of acquiring Newtown Harbour for the Crown. At this time the harbour was capable of accommodating up to 300 ships. It was a useful deepwater naval base, amid fears of French and Spanish invasion, but its major use was as a trading base. In 1305, for example, it was sending large quantities of corn to Berwick to feed King Edwards troops. Its prosperity was largely derived from trade, reflected in some of the street names, such as Gold Street and Silver Street, and it held a popular annual fair up till the 1850s.

It continued to prosper until the gradual silting up of the estuary made it impossible for large ships to enter. By 1836, it had been declared a 'rotten borough', had lost its two MPs and its mayor, and a government commission had reported that of the 68 residents, living in 14 poor cottages, none had sufficient intelligence to hold municipal office. Since that nadir there has been a rise in its prosperity. The church has been rebuilt, the town hall repaired and wildlife sanctuaries established. The National Trust owns much of the harbour area and there are several Sites of Special Scientific Interest.

Look out here for wild chamomile.

The path continues along the edge of the next two fields until it reaches Sandpits Farm and a small lane. Climb over the stile and turn right onto Pump Lane, go through the white, wooden gate, one of two gates on the lane, making it virtually traffic free.

This takes you through the hamlet of Five Houses. Although there are rather more than five now, three of the original houses are still here, easily distinguished by their thatched roofs.

At the end of Pump Lane, turn left along Five Houses Lane. At the crossroads go straight ahead along Quarry Lane to Newbridge.

From here you can see Tennyson Monument in the distance, atop the chalk downs. Just when you are getting fed up with walking along a road, you reach the village of Newbridge with its plethora of pretty,

Noah's Ark, formerly The Newtown Arms, the village pub

thatched cottages, blighted unfortunately by a not so pretty caravan park.

At the end of Quarry Lane turn left, then almost immediately right, over the Caul Bourne, the stream flowing north to Newtown harbour. Just after the bridge, turn right onto footpath S35, which follows the Caul Bourne to Shalfleet village.

After 200 yards the path emerges onto a small track.

The thatched building over to your right is the old mill farm. The track leads through Homestead Farm, a very good place to see swallows and martins, which nest in the barns here.

About 200 yards after the farm you will re-cross the line of the dismantled railway, now a farm track (if you look closely you can see traces of the embankment to your right). Just over the track, on your right, is a footpath which takes you down to the banks of the stream and is a delightful walk, at any time of the year, to Shalfleet, about three-quarters of a mile away.

When you eventually reach the village follow the little lane (Warlands Lane) round to the right of the church.

The lane is so called because of the attacks by the French who sailed into Newtown and up to Shalfleet. Parts of the church, including the tower, date back to the 11th Century and originally it had no entrance at ground level. This was done so that locals could use the church as a refuge during attacks. The walls are five feet thick and access was through a door in the roof. Like many local churches it had its own gun, kept in the tower, but this was sold, along with the bells, early in the twentieth century to pay for repairs to the church tower.

*At the end of the lane cross the main road and go down Mill Road, opposite, passing the New Inn and Shalfleet Manor Farm on your left. When you reach the 'dead end' sign bear right to continue down Mill Road. Go past Shalfleet Mill, which is mentioned in the Domesday Book, and over the footbridge. Follow the footpath through the copse, which is marked with yellow arrows, then turn left onto a tarmaced drive for about 300 yards. This emerges on Corf Road, next to Corf

Farm. Turn left and walk along the road for about 200 yards. Shortly after the sign for Corf Scout Camp go through a kissing gate into the field on your left, next to the road, and take the permissive path which runs parallel to the road, all the way to the junction with Town Lane. Leave the field via another kissing gate and turn left into Town Lane. Walk back to Newtown over the Causeway Bridge and past the Old Town Hall to the car park.

The Lazy Cow, Three Gates Farm
Tel: 01983 531204

The Lazy Cow is open in the summer from 10am-4pm. In the spring and autumn they generally only open on sunny days as, rather unusually, they only have outdoor benches (they used to have a marquee but it blew down in a gale). So it may be worth ringing first if in any doubt. However, this does mean the staff aren't too worried about muddy boots or bikes, and they can't tell you to leave your dog outside!

It is very friendly and the staff are passionate about good quality food. The café serves generous helpings of homemade cakes, made using good quality ingredients, and the cream teas use fresh Isle of Wight clotted cream, or try the superb Calbourne Classics ice-cream. Tea is served in metal tea pots with no-nonsense china, all quite suitable for outdoor tables, giving a relaxed, almost picnic feel to the experience. Great for a sunny, summer afternoon.

Next to the café is Three Gates Farm shop which is open every day, 10am to 4pm, selling a range of local produce, including the ice-cream, if you want to take some home with you, and sometimes takeaway cakes. So even if the café is not open you could still get some nibbles.

Dairy Deli Café
Tel: 01983 531557

Although not directly on the walk route, this nearby delicatessen has a few tables and serves good quality teas and coffees. The cake selection is generally limited to two or three choices from the Calbourne Classics range so they are always very fresh. Service is attentive and pleasant.

Walk 21:
Gurnard Marsh and Thorness

Footpaths and road with several stiles. Cliff edge walk good with stunning views (subject to coastal erosion). This walk could be combined with the following walk, see walk 20 for further details.

Distance	3½ miles/5.5km
Start	The Little Gloster car park
Parking	Park in The Little Gloster car park, if you will be visiting there later, or in the road nearby
Getting there by car	Gurnard is just off the B3325 to the west of Cowes. Marsh Road is at the western end of the village
Getting there by bus	Unfortunately the number 30 bus, past here, only runs twice a day. Otherwise the nearest bus route is the Number 32, which stops at the Portland Inn. You will then have a half mile walk along Worsley Road and down Solent View Road onto the Marsh. Check times with Wightbus

From the car park head west. Cross over the Luck, the stream flowing out to the Solent, at high tide a very picturesque sight, with its pretty, bobbing boats. Follow the short path along the western side of the stream to the stile, which leads on to the cliff edge.

Here you will have a beautiful view across the Solent to the New Forest and the Beaulieu River, almost opposite. On a clear day, you can see as far east as Portsmouth and the South Downs, and as far west as Hurst Castle, built by Henry VIII to defend the Solent..

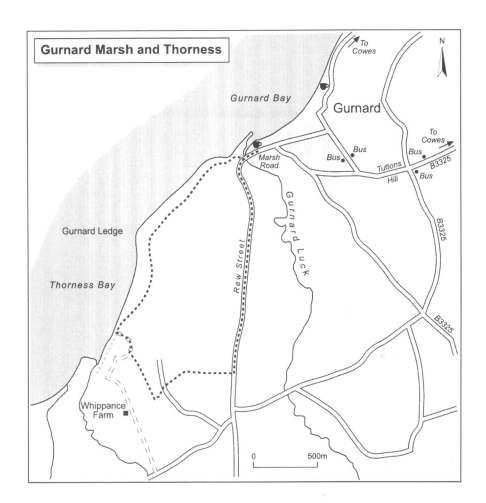

Carry on for just over a mile until you begin to descend into Thorness Bay and can see the holiday camp ahead of you.

The foreshore below is a haven for wildlife and at low tide the long spits are good places to find small fossils. On this side of the valley are older, privately owned, holiday chalets, some of which are converted railway carriages from the 1960s. When the railway lines were closed down it was cheaper to sell them off on the Island than to ship them back to the mainland.

When you reach the designated open access area take the path to the left, round the outside of the field, in front of the chalets, one of which is decorated with shells. Turn left after 'Manyana', opposite the stile. The path goes down the side of 'No.57'.

Cross the next stile and continue straight ahead, alongside the hedge, over two more stiles, then the path turns left into a copse. After a short distance, the path joins a concrete track for 50 yards. At the finger posts, go over the next stile and straight ahead, following the sign to Rew Street. This path curves round past Sticelett Farm. When you reach the road, turn left and follow it for just over a mile, back to Marsh Road.

This little area, known as Gurnard Marsh, consisting mostly of chalet type buildings, was once a separate little hamlet. Most of the chalets were built as temporary holiday homes, and had no running water or mains electricity. Under local regulations they could only be lived in for

View across fields to Thorness Bay

part of the year. Most have been improved over the years and many are lived in all year round, but if you look carefully you will see some in their original condition – it is a strange phenomenon that these are much harder to see than the renovated ones. You may also notice that, because of the marsh, many are built on stilts. Gurnard Luck often breaches its banks, especially in winter, and anything here has to be able to tolerate salt spray at the very least, plants included.

The Little Gloster, Gurnard Marsh

Opening times:
Mondays: Closed (except Bank Holidays)
Tuesday* to Friday: 10:30am-10:30pm
Saturday: 9:00am-10:30pm
Sunday: 9:00am–6:00pm
*closed on the Tuesday following a bank holiday
Tel: 01983 298776

The café has fantastic views from the terrace across the Solent and is a great place to watch the sailing action in the summer. Tea is served in pots and the coffee is delicious. There is a small array of freshly made cakes. All the food, including the cakes, is made on the premises, often using locally-sourced ingredients, and service is friendly. They also have a bar if you want something a bit stronger and serve good lunches with an interesting menu. The head chef, Ben Cooke, has brought his experience of working on some of the premier super-yachts to the Isle of Wight. Although this is a new place its reputation is growing.

Walk 22:
Cowes and Gurnard

Local interest. Solent views. Easy walking, mostly on roads. First half suitable for wheelchairs. A very simple walk but with lots to see. This walk could be combined with the previous walk, beginning in Cowes then continue on to walk 19 when you reach the Water's Edge Café – instructions given.

Distance	3½ miles/5.5km
Start	The Parade in Cowes
Parking	There are plenty of places to park in Cowes
Getting there by car	Cowes is at the northernmost point of the island on the west bank of the River Medina
Getting there by bus	Bus number 1 from Newport

It is worth stopping for a moment to lean on the wall and look out over the busy harbour. In summer the moorings are full of yachts, mostly dayboats; the larger ones tend to be in the marinas. On the other side of the harbour is a hangar with a giant Union Jack, painted to commemorate the Queen's Silver Jubilee in 1977. A few years later it was going to be over-painted but was saved by a petition got up by a young schoolboy, so it stayed. From here, in June 1959, Saunders-Roe launched the 'SRN1', the first hovercraft, designed by Christopher Cockerel, down the slipway, to test it in the waters of the Solent. Saunders-Roe also designed and built 'The Princess' here, the largest flying boat ever made.

Cowes is most famous as the home of international yachting and has five yacht clubs, four of which are here on the Parade. The oldest, and best known, is the Royal Yacht Squadron (RYS) at the far end of the Parade, with its red and white canopy. It is based in one of the cowes or castles built by Henry VIII, from which the town gets its name.

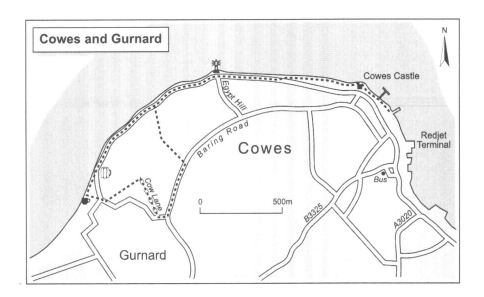

Despite the building work over the centuries, you can still see the battlements and sloping outer wall. The remains of the east cowe are visible on the headland, sticking out on the other side of the harbour, beyond the breakwater. The RYS has the reputation for being the most exclusive in the world, and is said to have turned down an application for membership from Sir Thomas Lipton, because he was 'only a grocer', despite him having spent a fortune challenging for the Americas Cup and not withstanding an appeal from King Edward VII.

It was from here that the first Americas Cup was sailed, round the Isle of Wight, and the cannons below the squadron walls are still used to start many races, including Cowes Week and the Fastnet. Although it began life in 1815 as an ordinary yacht club, it was created The Royal Yacht Squadron by William IV in 1833. It was intended that the yachts should sail together, as a 'squadron', and they were entitled to carry guns. They were expected to be willing to assist the navy in case of attack and hence are entitled to use the navy's white ensign, rather than the red one that most yachts use when not racing. Although I am not aware of any modern yachts attempting to carry guns, it would add a bit of spice to the normal Tuesday evening racing. In the early days there was quite an emphasis on signalling. As well as the more usual signal communications between vessels, the RYS signals included

Cowes Week

Cowes Week has traditionally been part of 'The Season', coming after Goodwood and before the 'Glorious 12th', when the grouse hunting begins. This has fixed the date as the week containing the first Tuesday in August, although it was moved in 2004 because of particularly bad tides and will be moved again in 2012 to avoid clashing with the Olympics.

The regatta's origins can be traced back to George IV's interest in sailing. The first race started at 09:30 on Thursday the 10th August 1826, some six years after George became King, with the prize of a "Gold Cup of the value of £100" and was held under the flag of the Royal Yacht Club, which later became the Royal Yacht Squadron. Another race was held the next day for prize money only; £30 for first place, £20 for second. Initially, Cowes Week included rowing and sailing races. But later, as sailing became more accessible to those with more modest incomes, it became sailing only. Cowes Week is now the largest sailing regatta in the world, hosting up to 2,000 yachts each year. It is an honour which has mixed blessings. While it is exciting to see so many yachts in such a relatively confined area and presents some challenging sailing to the competitors, the town has pretty much reached capacity. There simply isn't anywhere else for either boats or people to go. I can see a day coming when a 'FULL' sign will hang on the end of the breakwater.

The sailing is, for many, very competitive, but even as late as the 1990s other things like a tin bath race were a traditional part of the fun, and there are still always plenty of entertainments for the landlubbers. Although certain functions in the week are still the preserve of the elite or members-only clubs, Cowes Week includes plenty of events for everyone and the whole thing often seems like a week long party.

The attraction of Cowes Week has also given life to many water-based activities and sailing schools, promoting the sport of sailing to all age groups and walks of life in and around the town

The start of a yacht race

*such useful phrases to other yachts as, 'Can you lend me your band?'
and, to shore, 'Send me 300 oysters'.*

*During the summer, and especially during Cowes Week, it is not
uncommon to spot major and minor celebrities. Most members of the
Royal family have been here at some time or other and Prince Philip
was a keen competitor. There are, of course, the sailing stars like
yachtswoman Ellen McArthur and Double Olympic gold medallist
Shirley Robertson who live here. But there are also numerous others
who come for the sailing, such as Ben Ainslie, Simon Le Bon and
Geoffrey Hughes, and plenty who come for the partying. Princes
William and Harry had a well publicized jaunt here early in 2008, and
Lewis Hamilton took part in the Round the Island Race in June of that
year. So keep your eyes open!*

From the Parade walk north, under the castellated walls of the
Squadron to the esplanade, and continue on to Prince's Green.

At the entrance to the Green is Grantham Court, built on the site of Grantham House. Lord Grantham played a key role in the founding of the RYS, but a later resident of the house was GR Stephenson, son of the inventor of the steam engine. To commemorate a visit of the future Edward VII and his new bride, Princess Alexandra, Stephenson donated Prince's Green to the people of Cowes, on the condition that it should never be used for commercial purposes. Without this, it is likely that it would have been built on long before now. Instead, it has become a lovely place to watch the comings and goings in the Solent and is a very popular viewing place for Cowes Week, so thank you Mr Stephenson.

About 400 yards further along is an unusual sight; a house with castellations, called Rosetta Cottage, now owned and let by the National Trust. It is a pretty building whose main claim to fame is that Winston Churchill's parents met here in 1873. A little further on is Egypt Light, built in 1897, and opposite, the castellated Egypt House – castellation

Egypt House was supposedly built on the site of a gypsy camp from which it gets its name

must have been the fashion. The name 'Egypt' here probably derives from a camp of gypsies settled here in the 1700s, rather than the country. For decades the light provided a guide into the harbour, but wider use of radar and other technology meant that it was no longer needed, and it was decommissioned in 1989. Although at the time its loss was much criticized by local fishermen, the arrival of GPS has made it obsolete. In any case, there is so much lighting along the shore now, it is doubtful if it would still be visible.

The walk along Egypt Esplanade is a pleasant stroll with lots to look at. Watch out for cormorants flying only a few inches above the surface of the sea and the more delicate terns flying high, then diving head first into a shoal of fish, you may even see the occasional gannet. The furthest point of the walk is Gurnard Bay, with its traditional green beach huts, and this is the location of the Waters Edge Restaurant.

[To continue on to walk 19: On leaving the Water's Edge turn left and walk up the hill, Shore Road. After 100 yards, turn on to Winding Way on your right, walk the few yards up here to rejoin Shore Road above the bend. 200 yards further on, turn right into Solent View Road and walk down to the Outlook Café, where Walk 19 begins.]

To return to Cowes you can simply retrace your steps along the seafront. Somehow things look different in reverse. For those without pushchairs and the like, an alternative return route is up the hill next to The Woodvale pub. Just after the pub, on the left, are some steps (not the sloping path) to a path running behind the Woodvale. There is a footpath sign but it is often overhung by trees. Go up these then, after 30 yards, take the next left.

There are a lot of birds, including woodpeckers, in the little bit of copse that you pass, as well as red squirrels and foxes.

After 100 yards this path emerges in a small housing estate. Go straight along the road, looking for the path in the corner on your left, next to no.23. This leads into a small lane known as Cow Lane, which was a farm lane leading to footpaths across the fields until the seventies. At the end of the lane, turn left, then left again onto Baring Road. Walk along the road for 300 yards, then turn left down Battery Road, passing Brambles Lane. Where the road turns sharp left by no.18

there is a footpath straight ahead, which appears to go down the drive of No.22, but in fact leads past it and on into the copse encountered earlier, and another chance to see the elusive red squirrels.

This copse is a little gem of a wildlife haven which, although coveted by developers, has so far been preserved as the demarcation between Cowes and Gurnard. It has not been heavily managed either and, despite being used by generations of children to make dens, many parts remain pretty much untouched. There are plenty of wild flowers in the more open areas by the path and the 200 year old oaks play host to a variety of wildlife.

The path takes you back down to the Esplanade. Walk back along here to Cowes.

Gurnard Beach